# preparing him for the other woman

## Sheri Rose Shepherd

Multnomah Books

PREPARING HIM FOR THE OTHER WOMAN
published by Multnomah Books

© 2006 by Sheri Rose Shepherd
International Standard Book Number: 978-1-59052-657-6

Cover design by Kirk DouPonce, DogEaredDesign.com

Published in the United States by WaterBrook Multnomah, an imprint of the Crown Publishing
Group, a division of Random House Inc., New York.

MULTNOMAH and its mountain colophon are registered trademarks of Random House Inc.

Printed in the United States of America

For information:
MULTNOMAH BOOKS
12265 ORACLE BOULEVARD, SUITE 200 • COLORADO SPRINGS, CO 80921

Library of Congress Cataloging-in-Publication Data
Shepherd, Sheri Rose, 1961-
Preparing him for the other woman / Sheri Rose Shepherd.
  p. cm.
ISBN 1-59052-657-0
1. Mothers and sons—Religious aspects—Christianity. 2. Marriage—Religious
aspects—Christianity. 3. Christian education of boys. I. Title.
BV4529.18S535 2006
248.8'431—dc22

2006015538

14—10 9

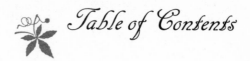 *Table of Contents*

# What Kind of Husband Will Your Son Grow Up to Be?

*I*t was a picture-perfect evening by the campfire on one of Southern California's beautiful beaches. My precious three-year-old son, Jake, and I were snuggled up under a blanket, watching the sun set over the ocean. The waves gently lapped the shore. A young couple walked past us hand in hand, obviously in love.

I'll never forget what happened next. My little boy thought for a minute, turned his sweet little face toward me, and said, "Mommy, will you marry me when I grow up?" It was one of those moments that will be engraved on my heart forever.

I gently explained to him that mommies can't marry their sons. My heart ached as I watched tears well up in his big blue eyes and roll slowly down his kissable, chubby cheeks.

How I treasure that memory. In that "mommy moment," I realized the vast influence God had given me in my son's life. That night I got down on my knees and made a promise to God that I would use whatever time He gave me with my son to prepare him to become a man who knows how to love a wife.

It has been fifteen years since that magical moment on the beach. My son is now eighteen, and my training time is nearing an end. We often talk about his future bride. Even though we do not know her name yet, we have been praying for her and preparing him to be her husband from the time he was a little boy.

## What Will Happen If We Do Nothing to Prepare Our Sons to Fight for Their Future Families?

I have spoken at countless women's events over the past two decades, and I can't tell you how often broken women have shared the same stories with me, over and over, about how empty their marriages are or how the marriage ended. Every time I came home from one of these conferences, I cried out to God to give our men the strength to fight for their families, remain faithful, and gain knowledge on how to love their wives and protect their families.

Then one day something occurred to me: The way a man loves a woman has a lot to do with what he learned as a little boy through his relationship with his mother. This is because she is the woman God placed in his life until he is married.

What if a husband had a mother who invested her life not only in cooking, cleaning, and caring for her son, but also in carefully and deliberately bestowing upon him what every man desires to know—how to understand and care for the fragile heart of his bride? What if every groom walked down the aisle with more than a ring and some heartfelt vows?

Imagine how differently many tragic love stories would end if every new bride took the hand of a well-trained hero— a strong warrior, equipped for victory as a loving leader. The marriage love story would be much more fulfilling if young princes were raised learning the art of loving their future wives.

## How Will You Prepare Your Son to Love a Wife and Lead a Family?

We are raising a generation of boys who have better relationships with their video games, iPods, televisions, and computers than they have with their families. Their world is one where pornography is no longer a hidden shame, but encouraged as entertainment. With a 50 percent divorce rate both inside and outside the church, this generation's view on marriage is that it has little hope for success.

Our sons are embroiled daily in a battle of the mind. They are being bombarded by conflicting messages about what a real man is. Today's so-called heroes are exalted for selfish pursuits—pleasure, money, and fame. It seems our sons are educated on every subject *except* how to love a wife and lead a family.

Far too few role models are willing to take a stand against immorality and infidelity, to teach our boys to declare victory for themselves and the generations to follow.

## This Book Is *Not* Meant as a Replacement for the Role a Father Plays in His Son's Life

We all know how important a godly, loving father is in a boy's life. You and your son are very blessed if you have a man of God in your home during these critical years.

But tragically, one in four homes today is without a man in the house at all, leaving many mothers alone in their battle to raise their beloved boys. Countless other homes have fathers who have relinquished their God-appointed role in their son's life. Too many of our boys grow up seeing ungodly, critical, or controlling behavior displayed by the man in their home, rather than witnessing the example of a good, strong, loving leader.

You as a mother cannot replace the father role in your son's life. However, you *can* raise a modern-day hero who will fight for his family and be a faithful, loving husband and father. Consider all the great men through history who attribute their success in life to their mother's influence and prayers.

I pray you will grab hold of this truth: Our God is the same today as when He raised up mighty men in a fallen world thousands of years ago. He is bigger than any statistic, any attack, or any circumstance you find yourself in. He is the lover of your soul; He is your provider; and ultimately, He is your son's Father.

God's intervention, combined with our prayers, training, and influence in our sons' lives, will help us empower and equip the next generation of men, their marriages, and their future families.

> *And she made this vow: "O LORD Almighty,*
> *if you will look down upon my sorrow*
> *and answer my prayer and give me a son,*
> *then I will give him back to you.*
> *He will be yours for his entire lifetime."*
>
> 1 SAMUEL 1:11, NLT

# chapter one

# Teach Him to Understand the Heart of a Woman

*In the same way, you husbands must give honor to your wives.*
*Treat her with understanding as you live together.*
*She may be weaker than you are, but she is your equal*
*partner in God's gift of new life. If you don't treat her*
*as you should, your prayers will not be heard.*

1 PETER 3:7, NLT

*O*ur God feels very strongly about men living with their wives in an understanding way. In fact, He made this conditional statement in 1 Peter 3:7: "If you don't treat her as you should, your prayers will not be heard."

Sounds like a simple command, doesn't it? Yet it is a distinct challenge for any man to put into action, considering we women are so complex that many times we do not even understand ourselves!

I have several Christian girlfriends who love their husbands yet feel alone in their marriages. They long for their husbands to tune in to their hearts and treat them with understanding rather than try to fix or change them. Now, I know these husbands—they are godly men who love their wives. Yet they often appear completely clueless when it comes to the instruction given in 1 Peter 3:7.

It's as if husbands grew up going to Man School. They have no trouble passing the "guy" courses: Acting Cool 101, Success and Achievement 102, and Sports 400. All of the skills learned in those classes come naturally, and are only reinforced through peer pressure.

On the other hand, while men often pass Getting the Girl 101, most guys flunk out of Understanding Women 101. Why? Because no one teaches this course in the school of married life!

Some men can turn to their own dads for help, but unfortunately, most fathers have the same diploma from Man School hanging on their walls.

Is it any wonder husbands everywhere feel frustrated and alone, trying to master something they were never trained for?

*Mother Teresa was once asked how we can restore peace to our world. Her answer was simple: "Go home and learn to love your family."*

Most of us cannot imagine the world-changing power of one man who has learned how to love, lead, and understand his wife and family.

In the 1990s, the Promise Keepers movement became a national phenomenon, with millions of men marching under one banner. Their cry was for restoration of America's families—starting with their own. Their founder, Coach Bill McCartney, influenced many men with a call to something far greater than business success. Money, prestige, and worldly acclaim held little value for Coach McCartney, who experienced a nearly destroyed marriage before discovering this life-changing truth: "If you want to know the true character of a man, look into his wife's face. Whatever he has invested or withheld can be seen in her eyes."

> *If you want to know the true character of a man, look into his wife's face. Whatever he has invested or withheld can be seen in her eyes.*

I have a father who loves being married…but who, sadly, has been divorced three times from women he deeply loved. Each time I watched him struggle to understand what went wrong.

I believe that when a man walks down the aisle and says

"I do," it is his every hope and intention that his marriage be "for life." I'm sure his sincere desire is to understand and take care of the beauty he has chosen as his wife. He longs to be her hero and lead her safely through life.

Yet many times a husband discovers he does not know how to accomplish his God-appointed mission in marriage. Eventually, his attempts at love, leadership, and even heroism miss their mark as his beauty withdraws emotionally from the very one she hoped would rescue her. Sadly, his wife eventually closes up her spirit in order to protect her heart from hurt. Intimacy, happiness, and hope wither into isolation, pain, and despair. Feeling helpless and frustrated, the man she longs for gives up trying.

The result is often an empty marriage, adultery, or divorce, and what began as a love story ends in tragedy.

## Life Happens

It was her wedding day, the glorious moment she had dreamed about all her life. There she stood, dressed all in white, ready to say "I do"…when her husband-to-be dropped a bomb on her heart. He looked into the eyes of his eighteen-year-old bride just hours before the wedding ceremony and confessed, "I can't do this. I am in love with another woman."

There she stood, alone, humiliated, and eight weeks

pregnant with a son. To make matters worse, she had nowhere to run: Marriage was her last hope for deliverance from her abusive father.

Like all women, my stepmother, Susie, longed to walk down the aisle with the ideals of love, security, and companionship waiting in a tux at the other end. Instead she found herself alone and scared, her life shattered. Her dream of being rescued and whisked away to a life of happily ever after turned into a nightmare of despair.

How could she possibly succeed at raising a child alone? She had never witnessed a healthy marriage or seen what a loving husband looks like. What hope did her son have of victory, with so much stacked against him?

With nowhere else to turn my stepmother took her pain and placed it at the feet of God, the true Father. And what blossomed in its place was a pure, selfless love and single-minded passion for her boy and his future.

As that child grew, he learned the true meaning of the word *self-sacrifice*. He saw firsthand how determined his mom was to prepare him to become a great husband. Is it any wonder that my stepbrother turned out to be a modern-day hero? Today he loves the Lord with all his heart and is a well-respected man of integrity. After twenty years spent serving our country, he left the military as a highly decorated officer.

My stepmom's mission was accomplished; her training to raise her son to love his wife succeeded. I have never witnessed a man more in love with or tuned in to his wife's and stepchildren's needs than my brother. He exemplifies Christ's love in his home every day.

How can God use broken hearts and lives as tools to train our sons to become godly husbands? The answer is this: Our Father in heaven has all we need to turn our pain into divine purpose and our despair into divine destiny for us and our beloved boys.

If God could use Rahab the prostitute in the lineage of King David and King Jesus...if He could turn the sin of King David and Bathsheba into a son, King Solomon, who would become the wisest man who ever lived...then He can certainly use whatever you have done or whatever has been done to you to bring about something significant in your son's life.

Our boys do not have to become the lost generation that does not know how to love and lead a wife and family. Turn your heartache and disappointments into the passion you will need to raise a mighty warrior. Don't beat yourself up any longer for things gone wrong. Instead, use the mistakes made in your own marriage or relationships with men as tutorials. Teach your son what it takes to build a healthy, loving relationship with his future wife.

What saved my stepmom's son from becoming just another statistic is the power of prayer, the devotion of quality time, and the amazing influence a mom can have in her son's life.

## A Mother's Influence

A loving mother has the power to teach her son about the tender heart of a woman. Who better to show him how to truly appreciate the way a woman is wired by God Himself?

The time to prepare our boys is now. By using the weapons available to us—our undying love for them, our available time with them, our incomparable influence over them, and our powerful prayers—we can train them to become tender warriors.

God entrusts our beloved sons to us for only a certain number of days. What a great opportunity to invest in their futures by preparing them to love and understand the heart of their future wife.

## A Mother in Action

*Ages 3–8*
This age range—while your son desires your approval and attention—is the perfect time to teach him how to become a tender warrior and to understand a woman's heart.

1.  **Teach him to take responsibility.** This is your chance to train your son about matters of the heart. To become a great husband, he must take responsibility for the way he treats and relates to girls and mommies. When your son does something to hurt you or any girl, don't make

excuses for him; instead, show him what taking responsibility for his actions looks like.

Many times I taught my son to take responsibility by using word pictures that required a response on his part. For example, "If Mommy accidentally drops a hammer on your toe and it hurts you, do I still have to say I'm sorry? Even if I didn't do it on purpose?"

2. **Talk about the power of his words.** Kids can be cruel to one another. You've heard the phrase, "Sticks and stones may break my bones, but words will never hurt me"— and you know how untrue it is. Words have the power to hurt or heal, build up or tear down. Look for opportunities to talk to him about the effect his words have on others.

3. **Be honest with him about how women think and feel.** I am not talking about turning your son into a man who thinks and acts like a girl. Rather, this step is about preparing him now for one of the greatest challenges he will ever face: understanding that his words and actions have the power to either hurt or heal a woman's heart.

Think about all the marriages you've seen in which women are hurting and their husbands have no clue why or how to heal their hearts. This lack of understanding leaves wives wounded, and a wounded wife is not a good thing in a marriage.

4. **Help him understand about gender differences.** God made girls more naturally tenderhearted than boys. Explain to your son that is why girls get their feelings hurt more easily. Help him understand that He made boys tougher so they can protect girls' hearts and emotions.

*Ages 9–13*
Continue to apply all the above and add the following:

1. **Keep training him.** During this time your son may not seem interested in matters of the heart. But believe me, he is watching and learning more than you realize. Don't give up on your training. Boys do a lot of things at this stage in their lives that hurt moms' and girls' feelings without realizing it. Be on the lookout for those vulnerable teaching moments.
2. **Validate his feelings.** The Word of God says to be angry, yet not sin. There are more than two thousand references in the Bible to the emotions of God. Do not shut your son down; rather, teach him to understand what he is feeling and how to work through it.
3. **Let him know you understand his heart.** Every son wants to feel understood and related to. He will learn the most about how to minister to a woman's heart through the way you minister to him, so take the time to tune in and hear his heart.

4.  **Pray with him when he is hurting.** By taking the time to pray with your son, you are training him now to always turn to his heavenly Father for healing, hope, and guidance. Someday he will teach that habit to his own children.

### Ages 14–19

The teenage years are the most opportune time to teach sons about tuning in to a woman's heart. Continue to apply all the above and add the following:

1.  **Take advantage of this time.** By this age he is attracted to girls but has relatively little idea how to sort out his feelings—let alone understand the strange and confusing emotions of girls! Take notice every time your son has a crush on a girl; let him know you are there to help him understand her heart.
2.  **Get him to tune in to his own heart.** The majority of husbands out there do not tune in to their wives' hearts because they don't understand their *own* feelings and emotions. They were taught by society that being strong means shutting down their feelings.

    Yes, men are hardwired to be strong; however, they also need to be sensitive to matters of the heart in order to become mighty men of God. King David was just as strong and mighty in understanding matters of the heart as he was in his manhood and faith.

When my son is emotionally hurt, I try to get him to recognize and talk about his feelings. When he is struggling to understand the actions or reactions of a girl he likes, we discuss it and I offer a woman's point of view on the matter.

3. **Try to keep it lighthearted, yet real.** Be honest and relatable when talking to your son about girls. If you want him to open up, start off with an intriguing comment like, "I know something about girls that you don't…!" That usually does the trick.

   Sometimes when I am teaching my son Jake about how women think, he'll get a perplexed look on his face and then blurt out, "Women are so bizarre!" My response is usually, "Well, men are emotionally challenged!" We have a lot of fun laughing together about the differences between men and women.

4. **Never make him feel stupid about things he does not understand.** If you do, you will lose your influence. Be a good listener, and get directly to the point when you have an answer.

5. **Relate to him through popular culture.** When things happen in his life with girls that he just does not "get," try to talk to him about it on his level. Using an illustration from a popular "chick flick" can be a valuable tool in helping him understand how women feel and think.

6. **Don't make male-bashing comments.** Many women who have been hurt by men are bitter and pass this negativity on to their sons. Eventually, the mothers lose their credibility, and the emotional connection with their sons is lost. Remember, all of this may not come naturally for your son, so be patient and positive as you enter with him into the world of girls.

7. **Get him to think about the girl's feelings.** If you can help your son do this rather than trying to fix her problems, you will be aiding him in a big way. This is one of the keys to tenderness with his future wife—whether he can relate to her or not.

   Ask him probing questions like, "What do you think she was feeling when she said that?" When your young man makes an effort to see things from a girl's point of view, he is well on his way to being a loving leader.

8. **Have him pray.** When your son is struggling to understand you, his sister, or his female friends, encourage him to stop and pray for guidance. Remind him that God created women and that He promises us wisdom if we ask for it—even about something as mysterious as the mind of a woman!

   If your son is uncomfortable praying about the issue, don't force it. Instead, offer to pray for him. As he grows in faith and maturity, he'll begin taking the initiative of a leader.

9. **Affirm him.** When your son does something to show that he loves and understands you, let him know how much it means to you. Tell him what an understanding husband he will make someday. Speak life into his future marriage with love notes, words of praise, and affirming actions.

10. **Teach him that women get their feelings hurt easily.** Here is my favorite illustration on this subject: When you hit someone with a two-by-four—whether you did it on purpose or by accident—*the pain is still real.*

11. **Help him tune in to his own heart.** Train your son to recognize his own emotions as well as the emotions of others. You do not want to put the pressure on his future wife to spend many frustrating years of their marriage retraining your son to tune in to her heart.

## The Big Picture

I always tell my son that I want to bless my future daughter in-law with a man who knows how to stay tuned in to her heart and how to handle problems in their marriage.

Think about all the husbands out there who are more tuned in to their TVs and the Internet than their own wives. Many men care more about their favorite sports team than the condition of their families.

In these situations, when the husband tunes out, the wife inevitably shuts down. When this happens, everyone suffers because the family loses its sense of connection to each other.

You are giving your son a great gift by helping him understand the need to be tuned in for his someday wife. You can bless your daughter-in-law immeasurably with a husband who is willing—and desires—to hear her heart.

*In this same way, husbands ought to love their*
*wives as their own bodies.*
*He who loves his wife loves himself.*

EPHESIANS 5:28, NIV

*A Mother's Prayer
for Understanding*

⌒

Dear God,

Help me remember that I am raising

someone's future husband.

I am with him for such a short time.

Please give me the wisdom

I need to prepare him to love his wife

the way You intended.

Give my son a heart of understanding, Lord.

Help him grow strong in his faith

and tender in his heart. Protect him from

the moral decay in this world.

Plant in him the desire to seek You

for guidance and to grow into a godly man.

In Your name I pray, amen.

# chapter two

# Teach Him to
# Become a Hero

*I have fought a good fight, I have finished the race, and I have
remained faithful. And now the prize awaits me—the crown of
righteousness that the Lord, the righteous Judge, will give me on that
great day of his return. And the prize is not just for me but for all
who eagerly look forward to his glorious return.*

2 TIMOTHY 4:7–8, NLT

 *I* decided when my son was very
young to face the world with him head-on, rather than hide
and pretend evil does not exist. If you shelter your son from
the real world, he will not find himself equipped with the
wisdom, strength, or stamina for the battles he will someday
face on his own. How can he become a strong and mighty
warrior for God's kingdom if he is never given the chance to
fight?

The fact is, our boys were *created* to fight battles.
Whether the attacker is a physical or spiritual entity, boys are

hardwired by divine design with the ability to protect their wives, their families, and their country.

Look at all the mighty men in Scripture who fought great battles and rescued or changed nations. King David was just a boy when he stepped onto his first battlefield—but he recognized a battle worth fighting for. His faith in God made him a true hero.

Can you imagine how King David's life might have turned out if his mother had run onto the battlefield and begged the giant not to hurt her baby? Or if she had taken matters into her own hands and attacked the enemy herself? David would never have had the chance to experience the Lord's strength in him. And he probably would not have completed his mighty work here on earth (not to mention the humiliation he would have endured as a result of his mother's intervention!).

## Life Happens

From the time my son Jake was two, we have prayed together that God will reveal opportunities for divine appointments. And time after time, God has used Jacob to be a hero in someone's life.

A few years ago we lived in a small Central Oregon town that had no mall. One day around Christmastime Jake and I drove to Portland for a shopping spree. Our Christmas shopping was done; we had been saving money for months to spend on one big day in retail heaven.

As we drove north, I had Jake pray for a divine appointment that day. And let me tell you—God didn't waste any time answering that prayer!

After parking the car, we headed into a computer store at the mall. Through one of the full-length windows at the front of the store, I spotted a young girl curled up on a bench, shaking. It was freezing outside, and she did not appear to have a coat. I couldn't see her face, but I could tell that she was in physical and emotional pain. My heart broke for her.

Tentatively, I walked outside and approached the girl. I asked her, "May I have the privilege of praying for you?"

To my surprise, she totally mocked me with a disdainful, *"Whatever!"*

I could see fear and defeat beneath her angry exterior, and I managed to stand my ground. I told her, "I'm not leaving you until I pray for you."

She clearly had neither the strength nor the will to fight with me. The most she could do was muster a defiant glare and shoot back, "Go ahead and get it over with."

I gently placed my hand on her shoulder and began to pray:

*Dear God, I don't know what this girl has been through, but You do, so please let her know today that You love her and that You can and will provide whatever it is she needs. In Your name I pray, amen.*

Jake saw me praying over the girl and came out to see what was going on. He witnessed the hardened shell around this young girl's heart soften as she began to cry uncontrollably.

When I finished praying, the girl began to share her story through her tears. She had gotten pregnant and her parents had kicked her out of their house because she refused to get an abortion. She desperately wanted to marry her boyfriend—the father of her baby—but they didn't even have enough money for a marriage license, let alone what it cost to raise a child. For months they had been living under a bridge. That very day her grief and pain had reached a pinnacle because she had given up her newborn for adoption.

Just then, the young girl's boyfriend walked up with some scraps of food he had found for their dinner. After an awkward introduction, my son blurted out, "Mom, it's time to shop."

I turned to him in astonishment and said under my breath, "Jake, didn't you hear their situation?"

He said, "Yes, Mom! It's time to take *them* shopping!"

For the next two hours, my fifteen-year-old son turned into a teenage superhero. He took the young man and bought him clothes, a sleeping bag, new shoes, and a backpack—all with his own money. I took the young girl with me and did the same.

At the end of our day, we got to pray the prayer of salvation with them—the greatest prayer of all.

As Jake and I drove home without any shopping bags in our car, Jake told me, "Mom, that was the best day I have ever had!"

At that moment I realized something of great consequence: The greatest battle our boys will ever fight is the desire to please themselves. When Jake is old, he will probably not remember many of the things I bought him. But he will *always* remember the day he was a hero in someone's life. Jake and I still pray together that the Lord will send him divine appointments.

Try not to overlook any opportunities for your son to be someone's hero.

## A Mother's Influence

Encourage your son's God-given desire for heroism and adventure! Boys need to be esteemed for their courage and strength. Our goal as mothers should be to teach and inspire them to fight for the things in life worth fighting for, and to help them find their courage and strength in the Lord.

Think of these years of training like a fire drill at school—practice for the real thing. Your son may not experience the real fire of his faith until he is married and caught in a real-life blaze. But if you prepare him now, he will be equipped then to save his family.

Most boys need to understand and experience how something works before they believe it. Real-life opportunities and divine appointments are everywhere. We as moms need to be ready and available to teach our sons how to be godly heroes.

## A Mother in Action

*Ages 3–8*

Teachable adventures present themselves every day. Encourage your young warrior to become a hero by looking for opportunities.

1. **Read to him.** Boys have fantastic imaginations and love to envision themselves as the hero. Adventure stories about exploration, discovery, courage, and victory over evil are great for bringing out the superhero in every small boy.

2. **Rent a movie that stimulates conversation.** Heroic themes really resonate with boys. An excellent choice is a movie like *The Princess Bride,* which contains both adventure and comic relief, yet paints a vivid picture of heroic love.

3. **Help him fight the good fight.** When you see him "pretend fighting," ask your little warrior to define *who* and *what* he's fighting for. Then offer compliments that are sure to make him proud, such as "You are so brave!" and "What a strong young hero!" If you continue to affirm him, you may discover that he enjoys rescuing princesses…including his mommy.

4. **Share a great Bible hero story.** God always shows up on the scene to give victory over the "bad guys." Teach your son about the historic victories of the Bible and watch him get excited about being a young warrior for God.

## Ages 9–13

Continue all of the above teaching and add the following:

1. **Cheer him on.** Keep your son active but don't force him into sports or other activities that he shows little interest in. It is your job to champion him in whatever he's interested in. That may be sports, music, art, or building things. Keep your eyes open as he explores his gifts and talents, and always support his interests. Heroes do their best with a cheerleader on their side.

2. **Stay tuned in.** When your son turns nine or ten, it is natural for him to start breaking away and exploring independence. It may seem like he is no longer the little boy who longs to be by your side every minute of the day.

   Many moms find it hard to stay close to their sons when they reach this age; they feel rejected or not needed as much. Trust me, he needs you close by and accessible—even as he is exploring the expanded new territory you give him. If you want to remain an influence in his life, you need to respect his space but stay tuned in.

3. **Foster his sense of adventure.** Part of staying tuned in is sensing when to be his cheerleader and when to join your son in his adventure.

   Too many moms squelch their son's need for adventure or choose to disengage rather than experience it alongside him. I'm not saying you should take up skateboarding, but great things will happen if you can join your son's Galactic Guy World of wonder. You will build a stronger, deeper relationship with him, and you can still monitor the influences being absorbed into his mind. The result is more opportunities for teachable moments without leaving him feeling like you've invaded his space. So build Legos with him, go bowling, or play pool. Anything that connects both of you is good.

4. **Join him in his world.** When my son grew interested in the high-tech world, I asked him to teach me how to play one of his computer games. Boys love to teach girls stuff, and it is an excellent way for them to get a taste of real leadership. If you can step into your son's world—even if you have little real interest in learning how to master an X-Box controller—you will come away with something greater: a stronger connection with your son.

*Ages 14–19*

Continue all the above teaching and add the following:

1.  **Seek to understand his daily battles.** There are giants all around our boys—drugs, sexual temptation, and peer pressure, to name just a few.

    Our teen sons experience an inner war every day while trying to figure out who they are, what they really believe, and how they fit into the world around them.

    If God could give a young boy on a battlefield the courage to stand up to Goliath—a giant that not even the most well-trained soldiers were willing to fight— then he can give your son the same courageous spirit to become a hero on his high school campus. When boys discover they are really warriors for God, they tap into the same strength David needed to conquer Goliath.

2.  **Train him for the battle at home.** King David's training for the great call on his life started when he was a child. It was at home that he learned to protect and lead while shepherding a flock of sheep.

    Most teens' worlds revolve around their friends. However, many bad choices happen during the high school years, when boys are old enough to desire independence but still aren't equipped to handle freedom. My son loves being with his friends, so we decided early on to make our house into a home that is inviting to teens. If it interferes with my décor, I remind myself that

I have the rest of my life to decorate—but limited time with my son.

3. **Take out the "trash."** We have a pool table in our living room, a Ping-Pong table in our garage, and a big-screen TV with a library full of good DVDs. However, there are two modern conveniences my husband and I have chosen to keep out of our home: the Internet and cable television.

Unfortunately, too many families would rather give up their microwave or indoor plumbing than live without the polluted river of media spilling into their homes. Believe me when I tell you this: Nothing will do more to undermine the development of true heroism that you want to instill in your son than a steady stream of trashy TV shows. Television steals the precious time we have to prepare our sons for life's battles.

Now, I'm certainly not saying that all television is bad. In fact, my Jewish family came to know the Lord through Christian television. But here's how I look at it: Why should Steve and I willingly pay for cable television when the vast majority of what's offered stands for everything we don't?

Another great thing about not having Internet or cable TV is that the money we save can be invested in table games that encourage relationships and healthy competition, rather than garbage for their impressionable minds.

4. **Introduce him to his Father in heaven.** Although David's earthly father, Jesse, never told his son that he would become a great leader, David's close relationship with his heavenly Father made him a hero. That intimacy gave the future king confidence to walk out on a battlefield and defeat a giant. Eventually, his love for his Father in heaven helped him become a great king.

5. **Help him gain God confidence.** Our boys don't need self-confidence to become true heroes; they need God confidence. King David's confidence was in his God, not himself. It was that devout confidence that strengthened him to persevere through the many trials he would face before becoming king.

   If you want to help your son understand who he is in Christ and prepare him to be a hero in his home, you need to point him to God, the hero maker.

6. **Help him see himself as a hero in his high school.** Boys don't have to do a whole lot in this day and age to become a hero on their high school campus. Don't overwhelm your son with unrealistic expectations that could set him up for failure—he may give up trying altogether.

   Instead, help him set obtainable goals. Inspire him to be strong and courageous by helping him see himself as the shepherd (leader) of his flock (friends).

   When one of his friends is in trouble, encourage your son to come up with a plan, then gently offer your wisdom or share a story about a time you experienced something similar. After you have discussed the situation in a thoughtful and concise manner, have your son pray with you for God's help.

7. **Listen with understanding.** This gets your son thinking about ways he might come to someone else's rescue or do the right thing. Follow up by sealing the situation in prayer, and you will give him the power he needs to become a great man of God. You'll have shown him how to think for himself, be proactive, and seek God for strength and wisdom. Combined, these qualities equal a true hero.

## The Big Picture

Too many men do not know how to be the hero in their wife's life. So what do they do? Ignore her cries for help, thinking that in the long run it will all work out. As a result, too many wives feel anything *but* rescued by the man they love.

Thankfully, it does not have to be this way. You can teach your son to put out the fires in his marriage before they get out of control. Our God is the same today as He was thousands of years ago. In other words, don't wait for the world to change its moral fiber; with God's help, you can raise a modern-day hero who will fight for his family and remain a faithful, loving husband and father.

All of God's children are called to be world changers. Let's stand together against the giants in our land and say, "As for me and my house, we will serve the Lord."

*For when your faith is tested,*
*your endurance has a chance to grow.*
*So let it grow, for when your endurance*
*is fully developed, you will be strong*
*in character and ready for anything.*

JAMES 1:3–4, NLT

## A Mother's Prayer

Dear God,

I pray You will give my son

the heart of a hero.

Give him the desire to do

something great for Your kingdom.

Help him fight the good fight

and keep his faith strong.

May he finish the race and

win many people for Your kingdom.

Inspire him, Lord, to fulfill

Your destiny for him.

In Your name I pray, amen.

# chapter three

# Teach Him to Express Love

*How sweet is your love, my treasure, my bride!*
*How much better it is than wine!*
*Your perfume is more fragrant*
*than the richest of spices.*
*Your lips, my bride, are as sweet as honey.*

SONG OF SOLOMON 4:10–11, NLT

*M*ost women would do almost anything to have their husband show them love like when they were dating.

Our heavenly Father understands a woman's desire to feel loved by her husband. He also knows the passion that burns inside a man for a woman. After all, He created that kind of love!

Unfortunately, few Christian marriages experience love the way God intended. Many men show more interest in and passion for their favorite sports teams or their jobs than their

41

own wives. And women everywhere are substituting their God-given desire for love with chocolate, romantic novels, and movies—anything to fill the void in their marriages.

We have settled for second best in marriage.

*We have settled for second best in marriage.*

Many well-intentioned Christian leaders and marriage counselors have led men and woman to believe that romantic expressions of love are only for the movies, not real life. This has perpetuated the lie that it is acceptable for men to emotionally vacate marriages and stop expressing acts of love. The irony of this is that Hollywood did not create the love stories that cause women to desire romantic love; it was our Creator who wired us to crave the affection of our husbands.

The truth is that our God wants to see "adoring love" expressed between a husband and wife. Whoever is teaching the church that romantic love is not God's will for marriage has never read the following verses from the Song of Solomon:

How beautiful you are, my beloved, how beautiful! Your eyes behind your veil are like doves. Your hair falls in waves, like a flock of goats frisking down the slopes of Gilead. Your teeth are as white as sheep, newly shorn and washed. They are perfectly matched; not one is missing. Your lips are like a ribbon of scarlet. Oh, how beautiful your mouth! Your cheeks behind your veil are like pomegranate halves—lovely and delicious.

Song of Solomon 4:1–3, NLT

## Life Happens

For the first seven years of our marriage, Steve and I appeared to be the perfect match.

We both love the Lord; we attend church together and love being in ministry. We eat healthfully and exercise regularly, we write books together, and we love being parents.

But the hidden truth was that during our first seven years as husband and wife, our marriage was nothing more than a well-decorated wedding cake: pretty on the outside, but completely lacking in flavor. In fact, I often felt more alone after marrying Steve than when I was single. I spent much of those first seven years only pretending to be happy.

Even though I knew Steve loved me, I didn't feel close to him. Why? *Because he hadn't been taught to express love to me, as a woman, in the way I needed him to.*

Finally one night I broke down. I told Steve I needed him to fill my love tank—that I had been running on empty for a long time. Unfortunately, Steve did not have the first idea how to fill me back up, so he did what many men do: He ignored his wife's cry for love.

After a while, I grew tired of waiting for my prince to rescue me from my pit of despair and cure my loneliness. Eventually, I shut down completely. I lost all desire for his affection. I built a wall of resentment so high and thick it would have taken a bulldozer to break it down.

In response, Steve became extremely critical and controlling in his efforts to penetrate the wall I had built around my heart. But it did not help. I was paralyzed by my pain. Needless to say, this left our marriage wide open for the enemy's trap.

Eventually, temptation knocked at the door of my heart in the form of another man—a friend that Steve and I had led to the Lord. This man spoke words that opened the door of my heart; he broke down walls I had been hiding behind. He never put me down or made me feel stupid for things I felt or thought. I could share my deepest feelings and biggest dreams with him. He showed me the kind of love that I longed for in my marriage to Steve.

For three months we carried on an affair of the heart over the phone. For the first time in seven years I felt truly loved.

This kind of love had so much influence over my life that I almost gave up all I cherished—my marriage, my ministry, and my dreams. Even though we never had a physical affair, I knew it was a sin. I could not stop; I was addicted to the attention he gave me.

Finally I cried out to God, and He used my husband to rescue me. Steve discovered my affair of the heart, but to my complete astonishment did not condemn me. Instead, he did something amazing: He came to me with tears in his eyes and roses in his hands and said, "This is my fault for not expressing how much I love you and making you feel safe and accepted."

Steve's expression of love that day did more than rescue me. It made him my hero and it saved our marriage. I am more in love with my husband now than ever. His extraordinary expression of love that day put me back where I really wanted to be all along: in his arms.

## A Mother's Influence

Most boys really love their moms and, if encouraged, want to express that love.

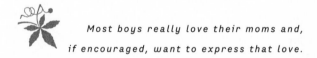

*Most boys really love their moms and, if encouraged, want to express that love.*

When I was forty and my son Jake was eleven, I got pregnant with his little sister. Needless to say, his world was rocked—especially when she was born very ill and needed much of my attention.

One day Jake happened to see me kneeling at the side of my bed, crying. He overheard me praying for a way to show him how much I still loved him.

The next thing I knew, I heard water running. Then my son came into my room and told me he had prepared a bath for me.

When I entered the bathroom I was rendered speechless. Candlelight flickered on the walls. A warm towel and robe, fresh from the dryer, were folded over a bench beside the tub. Jake had taped notes on the walls listing all the things he loved about me. As you can imagine, I found myself in tears and awe at the same time.

I share this story to remind you that a son's love comes from his heart. Don't be afraid to let your son see that you need his love—and then give him the chance to express it.

## A Mother in Action

*Ages 3–8*

1. **Make a big deal of his efforts.** The next time your son makes you a card or writes you a love note, let him know in a big way how he made you feel—even if he wrote it on your mirror in lipstick!

   The families richest in love, I've discovered, are those with plenty of "cha-chings" to go around. Let me explain: When my son expresses his love to me, I let him know how much I appreciate his efforts by saying, "Cha-ching!" In other words, "You just made a big deposit in my emotional bank account." Jake is eighteen now, and he still says "cha-ching" to me whenever I tell him how much I love him.

2. **Be affirming.** When your son expresses his love to you, be sure to say something like, "The girl who marries you will be the most blessed girl in the world!" If you affirm his future success as a great husband, he will believe it. And even more important, when he grows up he will *become* it.

3. **Snuggle up.** When your son wants to cuddle with you, stop whatever you are doing and savor that moment while you have the chance. If you are always too busy to snuggle with him, you send the wrong message that grown women do not need to be held.

     While you are cuddled up together on the couch, be sure to make comments like, "I'm going to miss this when you get big," and "When you get married some-day, your wife will love to cuddle with you." These are small but positive ways to make deposits in his "husband bank account."

*Ages 9–13 and 14–19:*
For both age groups, use the above teaching and then add the following:

1. **Keep loving on him.** Your son may not want to be as snuggly at this age as when he was little, but he still needs you to express love and affection to him—not forcefully, but with tenderness and sincerity.

2. **Do not miss the moment.** One thing I have discovered by having preteen and teen boys in my home every week is that they all long to feel loved. My son has friends who have no problem expressing love to their moms—or anyone else, for that matter. He also has friends (from both Christian and non-Christian homes) who have never felt comfortable hugging their parents or telling them, "I love you." Parents need to make time to express their love to their children.

3. **Have him tune in to you.** Encourage him to ask you every day, "How can I help you today, Mom?" This will get him in the habit of expressing love through acts of service. Think about how many men do not help around the house, and how may women feel taken advantage of rather than loved and cared for.

4. **Don't shut down.** As you know, most woman and girls naturally express love better than men. Therefore, it is important that you not stop offering expressions of love just because your preteen or teenager is beginning the natural process of distancing himself from you.

   Even if your son acts distant toward you, don't shut down. If you do, you run the risk of preventing him from expressing his love when he is ready. He will learn best how to connect with a woman through your example, so stay open to him. He still needs you to express your love and affection for him.

5. **Be straightforward with him.** When you want you son's attention, don't beat around the bush. The last thing he needs is for you to play mind games to get his attention—there is already too much manipulation being shown on television.

   Gently remind your son that you still need him to hug you once in a while, and then let him come to you. Write him a note of encouragement for his behavior or performance, or a thank-you for completing a certain chore or task.

6. **Continue showing him love, even when he does not reciprocate.** Remember that he still loves you, but at this point in his life he may not know how to express it. Remember that you are a woman, and women naturally express love better than men. Even when he does not respond, he is taking it in. Your example of unconditional love is teaching him how to love a wife.

7. **Affirm his actions.** When your son hugs you, kisses you, or tells you he loves you, let him know how much these gestures mean to you. But do *not* berate him for not expressing love at other times. Making him feel guilty—particularly after he has made an effort to express his love for you—will almost certainly ruin the moment and squelch future love gestures on his part.

8. **Use teachable moments.** When watching a movie together, point out scenes that demonstrate God-honoring expressions of love. Another good idea is to set up a weekly time for him to call his grandparents or handwrite them a letter telling them he loves them.

9. **Offer simple reminders.** Your son needs to be consistently reminded of positive ways to express love. Remember, he is male, so this will not come naturally to him. But if you consistently remind and gently affirm him, he will "get it" and become a loving husband someday.

## The Big Picture

How much better would all marriages be if husbands had been taught as boys to express the kind of love that reaches deep into their wives' hearts?

You are more than simply the mother in your son's life; you are also the representation of a woman's need to be loved. And the way you express love to him and teach him how to express love to you will greatly impact the way he loves his future wife and children.

The truth is, a Christian marriage should be the world's definitive expression of love. God even uses the marriage relationship as an illustration of His love for us, His bride. Yet sadly, I have heard countless young single adults and kids tell me they never want to get married because they are afraid they'll wind up as miserable as their parents.

You can avoid this by teaching your son about the value and importance of expressing love. Just think—you have the power to bless your future daughter-in-law with a husband who is not afraid to tell the world he loves her! Teach him to express his love in a language she can understand. Let him know how much you appreciate expressions of love like love notes, flowers, helping out around the house, words of affirmation, and tuning in to your emotions.

*Place me like a seal over your heart,*
*or like a seal on your arm.*
*For love is as strong as death,*
*and its jealousy is as enduring as the grave.*
*Love flashes like fire, the brightest kind of flame.*
*Many waters cannot quench love;*
*neither can rivers drown it.*
*If a man tried to buy love with*
*everything he owned,*
*his offer would be utterly despised.*

Song of Songs 8:6–7, nlt

## A Mother's Prayer

∽

Dear God,

I pray that my son will feel

free to express love to his wife someday.

I pray she will be the kind

of woman who knows how

to receive that love.

Help me teach my son to

love the way You desire him to.

Please grant him the strength

to save that love for his wife.

In Your name I pray, amen.

# chapter four

# Teach Him the Art of Affirmation

*The good man brings good things
out of the good stored up in him,
and the evil man brings evil things
out of the evil stored up in him.*

MATTHEW 12:35, NIV

Have you ever thought about how much your mother's voice—good or bad—stays with you over the years?

Now ask yourself this important question:

How does my son feel about himself after he has spent time talking to me?

According to the Word of God, the power of life and death is in our tongues. This means that your voice—your words—are among the most governing influences you have in your son's life. You can kill his confidence with just a few careless words, or you can speak life and truth by teaching him to affirm a family.

No one understood the power a parent has in a son's life better than the Jewish people in Bible times. They verbally and ceremonially spoke life to their sons as they passed the blessing to each new generation of young men.

Affirmation does not mean pretending our sons are perfect or faultless. But remember, God called Gideon to be a mighty warrior when he was hiding out and acting like a wimp. God sent Samuel to anoint and pray over the future King David years before that promise came to pass. I am sure Samuel's words of affirmation greatly helped David persevere through the many trials he had to face prior to assuming the throne.

Speak life to your son while he is with you, and then watch him blossom into a man of God.

# Life Happens

In high school I was sixty pounds overweight, addicted to drugs, a D-average student, and rebellious. However, my dad kept telling me I could become anything I wanted to. He constantly reminded me that I was destined for success.

At the time I didn't believe him; his words seemed insincere because I felt like such a failure. But looking back now, I clearly see how his verbal affirmation laid the foundation for rebuilding my life years later, when I was ready to make the necessary changes to become the best version of me.

Although my dad was not perfect and my parents have since divorced, I learned from him a valuable lesson about love: It is of paramount importance that you bless your child with words of encouragement, hope, and promise.

My father never doubted his daughter's ability to do something big with her life. In a way, he willed my future success into existence. He taught me that God's promises are more powerful than any mistakes we make.

Today, despite my lifelong struggle with dyslexia and a high school English teacher once telling me I was born to lose, I enjoy the privilege of passing the same gift on to many others. Just as my father did for me, I affirm and encourage thousands of women around the world through my books and conferences. I also learned from my father to bless my own children by telling them every day that God has amazing plans for their lives.

Give your dearly loved boy this same gift.

Let your words be your legacy, passed from generation to generation.

*Let your words be your legacy,
passed from generation to generation.*

Raise a young man who knows how to speak life to his future family and to a world that desperately needs to hear it.

## A Mother's Influence

When I first found out I was pregnant with a boy, I wondered how a "girly girl" like me would ever relate to a son. My big question was, "What will I talk about with him?"

In order to prepare myself, I began watching the interaction between moms and their young sons. The following observations really helped me connect with my own son.

One thing I observed was that moms who yelled at their sons from a distance had little to no control over them. (Grown men do not respond positively when we yell or nag, so what makes us think our boys will?) But the moms who took their boys by the hand and squatted down to eye level seemed to have a much better connection and command deeper respect from their sons.

## A Mother in Action

*Ages 3–8*

1. **Set the example.** The way you talk and listen to your son while he is young will have the biggest impact on his ability to master the art of affirmation.
2. **Engage him on his level.** Something else I noticed immediately was how attentively little boys listen to stories about adventures and exploration. Encourage him to choose books that are of interest to him—part of affirming is tuning in to others' interests. Engage him on his level and show him that you want to be part of his world.
3. **Make time for him.** If you are too busy to sit and talk with him or don't give him the opportunity to express his thoughts and feelings, he will eventually stop trying to communicate with you. This is one of the first stages of losing your connection to his heart.

   As a mother, be careful not to get too caught up in your to-do list. If you cut your son off every time he tries to tell you something, you'll wind up sacrificing this precious time in his life. An important part of affirmation is making time for him.

4. **Encourage his excitement.** Take every opportunity to engage him in dialogue, letting him know that the things that matter to him are important to you as well. Teach him that affirming words, eye contact, and active listening are all part of positive affirmation.

## Ages 9–13

Continue using all the above and add the following:

1. **Be careful what you say.** Let's face it: None of us say the right things all the time. But it is important to teach your son that what we say affects others. You know the saying, "A picture is worth a thousand words"? At this age, your son hears and processes far more than you may realize. Because of this, how you talk about men, church leaders, your friends, and family relatives are all leaving imprints in his mind that will last a lifetime.

2. **Teach him to ask questions.** Encourage him to ask about your day; this will train him to someday tune in to his wife's emotions and need for quality conversation.

Also, have him ask questions when he is talking to his sisters, brothers, or anyone else in your family. It is important that your son learn how to engage people in conversation. If you allow him to talk only about himself, he will not learn the importance of connecting with and showing interest in others.

3. **Let him hold you accountable for your conversations.** If you slander someone in front of your son, don't try to justify it; rather, apologize and then make it right. Say something like, "I should not have said that"—or even better, ask him to hold you accountable: "The next time you hear me say something mean about someone, will you tell me?" These kinds of conversations with your preteen will give you great influence in his life.

4. **Humble yourself.** Your son will be more respectful of your instruction regarding his conversations if you humble yourself and ask him to help hold you accountable for *your* words.

By doing this, you set a standard of excellence for your son. It shows him that Christians need to walk and talk in ways that are pleasing to our Father in heaven. My son is now eighteen, and I still ask him to hold me accountable if he perceives my words as gossiping or out of line.

### Ages 14–19
Continue using all the above and add the following:

1. **Talk to his friends.** I always ask Jake's teenage friends, "How is your relationship with your mom? Do you feel comfortable talking to her?" Their answers vary wildly.

Either they can talk to their moms about anything, or they have very little connection and they wish their moms would stop nagging them. This to me is an important reminder that our sons want mother figures who love and affirm them—whether they act like they do or not.

2. **Remove the distractions.** If you want to teach your teen son the art of communicating with a woman, seek his full attention by removing all distractions. This means that TVs and cell phones are turned off and your to-do list is temporarily laid aside. Simply put, it is too difficult for your son to hear you if your attention is divided.

3. **Be his conversational coach.** Women have a talent for conversation. Use this skill to teach your young man how to effectively express himself through dialogue. But remember, your words are not nearly as effective as the actions you live out.

4. **Be available.** Make it a priority to be available to your son whenever he is willing to open his heart to you. I have found in my own home that my son's friends really do want their mothers to speak their language and hear their hearts. Your availability to your son is an important way to affirm your love for him.

   Think about the long-term ramifications. What wife doesn't appreciate it when her husband makes time for her?

5. **Tune in to your son's world.** I am sure most of you remember your teen years and how your parents' words

bugged you sometimes. Many of you probably did not hear a word they said until you had moved out on your own and finally began to realize you did not have it all figured out.

The truth is, your teen needs to be listened to more than talked at. He wants to feel like you understand what he is going through.

6. **Ask questions.** Begin every conversation by asking your son about his day. Rather than "But did you...?" or "Why didn't you...?" responses, listen nonjudgmentally to find out what is in his heart. The teen years are difficult, and you need to stay tuned in if you want him to continue talking to you.

7. **Verbally affirm him.** Practice positive reinforcement when your son opens up to you. Try responding with, "Thank you for sharing your heart with me," or "Thank you for trusting me with that information." If you have something to add that relates to what he is saying, wait until he is done talking and then share it—but keep it short and sweet.

8. **Stop and listen.** I've spoken to hundreds of teens over the years, and the most important thing I've learned is that a son needs his mother's full attention. As soon as he walks in the door, try to get off the phone or the computer or wrap up whatever it is you're doing. In this way, you are telling him, *You are important to me.*

Giving him your undivided attention is an extremely effective way to affirm your son. When he responds with interactive dialogue, don't forget to thank him for sharing his heart. It will encourage him to do the same for his wife someday.

9. **Set a date with your son.** When you need to talk to your teenage son about something that's troubling you, invite him to coffee or out to dinner. He'll better hear you if he is prepared ahead of time.

Always begin with an affirmation, and then get directly to the point. Tell him why you are concerned and ask how you can encourage him in this area. Let him know that above all, you want to help him become a great husband someday.

10. **Don't be afraid to say, "I'm sorry."** If you embarrass your son or hurt his feelings, offer him a sincere apology. This affirms your love for him by validating his emotions.

11. **Be creative. It will pay off.** Other tools for teaching him to affirm others might be to write him a letter or text-message him on his cell phone. Do whatever it takes to stay connected; when he is grown, he will continue to cherish that connection with you and seek out your wisdom.

12. **Underscore constructive criticism with love.** When you talk to your son about a concern, use statements

like, "You have too much going for you to do this," or "You do not want to act like that—we both know it's not who you really are."

13. **Believe in him.** Every successful man throughout history had at least one person in his life who believed in him, who spoke his success into existence long before it came to be. The way you talk to your son will have a serious effect on the way he communicates with others—including his own wife someday. After all, positive communication is one of the key ingredients to a successful marriage.

*The way you talk to your son will have a serious effect on the way he communicates with others— including his own wife someday.*

## The Big Picture

There is nothing more wonderful to a woman than a man who uses his words to affirm her and their children. Unfortunately, fatherly affirmation is missing in the lives of many boys today.

I recently ran into a couple of my guy friends from high

school who had been raised by mothers in single-parent households. Whenever these boys hung out at our home, my stepmom, Susie, constantly affirmed them. She told them how successful they were going to be someday and what great husbands they would make.

Today these men are two of the most successful business-men in northern California, and they attribute a great deal of their success to Susie's affirmation. In fact, their wives have both written my stepmom letters thanking her for believing in their husbands.

History does not have to repeat itself. We can get down on our knees and pray to reverse the negative trends in this generation and speak words of affirmation into our sons' lives. Our boys can become positive, affirming husbands and fathers. Let's do our part to speak life into their lives *now*!

*He traveled through that area,*
*speaking many words of*
*encouragement to the people.*

ACTS 20:2, NIV

## A Mother's Prayer
## for Understanding

∽

Dear God,

Teach me to season my

conversation in a way that sets a positive

example for my son.

Help him speak words of life

and words of wisdom to his

friends and family.

Forgive me for anything

I have said to hurt my son.

Give him Your words when he talks,

and help him bring out the best in others.

In Your name I pray, amen.

# chapter five

# Teach Him to
# Resolve Conflict

*Most of all, love each other as if
your life depended on it.
Love makes up for practically anything.*

1 PETER 4:8, *THE MESSAGE*

*T*hink about what makes your heart melt when you watch a great love story. It's not the hero's physical strength or his beloved's beauty, is it? No, you and I are drawn to the power of true love and its inexplicable ability to prevail over tragedy and adversity. The greater the conflict, the stronger the love must be in order to reach resolve. When the hero does whatever it takes to save the relationship, our hearts soar with renewed hope.

That is just the kind of love we want to instill in our boys. We should be teaching them to fight for their marriages, *not* make excuses, blame others, and throw in the towel when conflict comes. Our goal as mothers should be to grow them into men who know how to fight *for* their families, not against them. Nobody wins at the blame game.

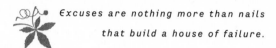

*Excuses are nothing more than nails that build a house of failure.*

We need to prepare our boys for the battles to come in every relationship. To do this, we must train them to fight the temptation to give up so they can win the war against broken marriages, broken hearts, and broken homes. There is no better way to show our sons what it takes to become a man of God than by teaching them the difference between right and wrong ways to handle conflict. I think a lot of men would fight for their marriages if only someone had taught them how.

I have observed many marriages over the years, and the most common sentiment I see in men is this: *Tell me how to fix it and I will.* Unfortunately, these men never had their mothers show them that women do not want to be fixed; they want to be loved and fought for. They want their husbands to take responsibility for the damage done by their words and actions. No woman can resist a loving, godly man with a humble heart and sincere apology.

## Life Happens

If there's one thing I observed growing up, it was how to fight loud and strong. My brother and I would hide out together in my bedroom as we listened to our parents rip each other apart during an argument, often screaming and throwing things at each other. These fights could last for hours.

I vividly recall certain images of them while they fought. My dad, red-faced, veins popping out of his neck, his hairpiece trembling like a little furry animal atop of his head, screaming at the top of his lungs, *"I want instant happiness in this home, and I demand it now!"* My poor mom, her eyes wide and round as saucers, the tears gushing as she screamed right back at him.

Sadly, that was the only kind of communication I knew growing up. Their fighting never did stop, and they divorced when I was thirteen.

To my poor husband, Steve, this kind of combat training was completely foreign. Steve was raised in quieter surroundings and not exposed to relational wars. His parents dealt with conflict quite differently from mine: No yelling. No broken furniture or flying utensils. In fact, his parents rarely fought at all—and never in front of their children. But his family also had no system for resolution. Silence ruled in their home when there was an issue to resolve.

Needless to say, Steve's and my fighting techniques were as different as night from day. Neither of us had been properly trained to handle marital conflict. You can imagine the challenges we experienced in our early years of marriage when we attempted to resolve a disagreement. During that time in our marriage, there was nothing teachable in either of our spirits.

To make things even more difficult, when I married Steve I was a brand-new Christian who had not yet learned how to channel my anger properly. So when Steve ignored our issues, I attempted to get his attention by screaming and crying. This made him close up even more, which led me to assume that he did not care about resolving our marriage problems. From where I stood, he *obviously* needed some lessons on how to express himself.

One day Steve's calm, cool responses made me so angry that I pushed him to the limit. I'd had enough of his "Let's work it out peacefully by ignoring our problems" act—in my mind, he was being polite only to irritate me.

I yelled at him, "Why don't you ever show some emotion and prove to me you care about our marriage?"

Steve stood quietly, but there was anger in his eyes.

"I would for once like to see you express your feelings about our problems!" I screamed.

Suddenly, Steve turned and released all his pent-up anger by kicking in the mirror on our bedroom closet door, smashing it to smithereens.

*Wow,* I thought, *what a performance. He sure learns fast.*

Suddenly I realized how stupid I was being. And just like that, my out-of-control rage turned to hysterical laughter. Then almost as quickly I began to sob. For the first time I understood how little we knew about effectively resolving conflict.

As he watched me helplessly, my poor husband winced in pain. His big toe was bleeding, his toenail jutting out at a bizarre angle. He asked me, "Is that enough emotion for you? If it would help, I could probably throw myself on the floor and work up a good cry."

I'm happy to tell you that Steve and I have become very good at confronting issues and moving past them quickly and effectively. We do not scream at each other, nor do we pretend that problems do not exist. Instead we work them out. It took several years, a lot of tears, and one expensive closet door mirror to repair the damage inflicted during those early years.

Today, after almost twenty years of marriage, we both joke that it's been the best six years of our lives. The rest of the time was spent learning how to resolve conflict without killing our love or affection for each other.

# A Mother's Influence

I used to think I could be the perfect Christian...if I never had to deal with difficult people.

God asks us to do our part in any and all situations and to live in peace with everyone. "If it is possible, as far as it depends on you, live at peace with everyone" (Romans 12:18, NIV). This means our family members, in-laws, spouses, friends, bosses, teachers, coaches—everyone!

However, God knows there may be people who are impossible to deal with, and He gives us an out: "If it is possible." We are His children, and we need to honor our Father in heaven by saying through our actions that His way is more important than proving our point to the person we are in conflict with.

*The next time you are in conflict, think of it as your cue from God to perform the miracle of reconciliation in front of your son.*

The next time you are in conflict, think of it as your cue from God to perform the miracle of reconciliation in front of your son. He will learn a great deal about relational conflict by watching you handle it.

# A Mother in Action

*Ages 3–8*

1.  **Speak truth to your son.** Let him know that every relationship experiences some level of conflict because we are imperfect people who say and do hurtful things. Than teach him that God's way is the only way to fix an argument or disagreement.
2.  **Ask him to pray.** When you are in an argument with your spouse or anyone else, do not be afraid to ask your son to pray for the situation. It is a great way to teach him to seek his heavenly Father first for help in the midst of conflict.
3.  **Thank him.** When the conflict is resolved, thank your son for his prayers and let him know how they helped. This will teach your son to have faith rather than fear when relationships encounter challenges.
4.  **Ask for his forgiveness.** If you say hurtful things to your husband or anyone else in front of your son, ask his forgiveness. If possible, let him witness the reconciliation; boys learn better by seeing something put into action than simply being told what to do.

*Ages 9–13*
Continue to apply all the above and add the following:

1. **Don't be too quick to come to his rescue.** When someone hurts your son, your first tendency as a mother will probably be to rescue him. However, if you study the Word you will find that every great biblical leader first had to endure many trials to prepare him for his God-given purpose.

   I have discovered in my own son's life that his future character is far more important than his comfort level. Sometimes life's trials are what a boy needs to become a man of character. Give him a little time to work through it before you step in and let him know you are there if he needs you.

*Sometimes life's trials are what a boy needs to become a man of character.*

2. **Help him depend on God more than you.** You will not always be there for him—but God will. Try not to fix all your son's problems before he has a chance to grow a little. Many times God reveals Himself to us when we are broken and cannot fix ourselves. Unless you are very careful, your good intentions may cause your beloved boy to depend more on you than God. If that happens,

he will not know how to think for himself or cry out to God when he encounters problems in life.

3. **Hear him out.** When your son is going through a relational challenge, hear him without interrupting. Allow him the freedom to vent. Validate his feelings, not his actions; then encourage him to think rationally.

4. **Let him come up with a resolution.** Ask him what he thinks he can do to fix the situation. His first response may be negative and defensive. Encourage him to look for a solution, not an out. Help him figure out how to grow from the conflict, and then gently add your wisdom and experience.

*Encourage him to look for a solution, not an out.*

5. **Have him pray.** After your son has expressed his feelings about the matter, teach him that only God can change his heart by having him pray for help to do the right thing. Keep in mind that your goal is to grow him into a godly husband who knows how to handle relational issues God's way, and in God's strength.

*Ages 14–19*

Continue all teaching from above and add the following:

1.  **Be real with him.** By "real," I mean relatable. Now, I am not suggesting you talk to your son like he is your therapist; you can be real without sharing every detail. But if you pretend your life is perfect and without conflict, this will do nothing to prepare your son for the challenges to come in his marriage relationship someday. Don't be afraid to discuss real-life challenges with your son; if you do, he will be much more willing to let you weigh in on his relational issues.

> *If you pretend your life is perfect and without conflict, this will do nothing to prepare your son for the challenges to come in his marriage.*

2.  **Make him take responsibility.** Teach your son now to take responsibility for his actions, regardless of the other person's actions or reactions. Encourage him to be proactive about bringing healing to the situation.

    The number one mistake a man can make in any relationship is to blame the woman. Even the first man to walk the earth blamed his wife, Eve, for the fall of man.

Preparing Him for the Other Woman

If you can get your son to look first at the role he plays, you will teach him to resolve conflict much more effectively. Remember Romans 12:18: "As far as it depends on you, live at peace with everyone."

*The first man to walk the earth blamed his wife, Eve, for the fall of man.*

3. **Deal with your relational issues.** This is a big one. If you have unresolved relational issues and your son sees that you are unwilling to forgive those who hurt you, he will do the same when he is grown and gone. On the other hand, if he sees that his mom knows how to deal with conflict, he will follow you down the road to reconciliation.

4. **Don't be too hard on him.** The Bible warns against exasperating our children, so be careful not to be too hard on your son while he is growing. When he does make a mistake in handling conflict, remind him of God's grace and mercy. We all make mistakes. High school, after all, is preparation for real-life relationships.

5. **Go privately.** The Word of God says that when you have a problem with someone, you should go to him privately and confront it. Teach your son to go privately to

whoever he is in conflict with by doing the same for him—that is, discussing important and personal matters privately. Nothing good will come of humiliating him publicly.

He will be exposed to enough humiliation in the real world; you need to be his safe place. Think how ugly it is when married couples point out each other's faults in front of others. Too much damage is incurred through those kinds of examples.

6. **Talk it out.** When your son offends someone through word or action, seize that teachable moment. Ask him how he thinks he should make it right; then stop talking and let him give his input. When he is through, ask him, "Can I offer you my thoughts?" Finally, close the conversation with a prayer. This will remind him how awesome God is at covering our hurtful words and helping us make things right, especially when we come to Him in prayer.

## The Big Picture

Look at how many men hop from woman to woman, hoping to find one without any problems or issues. Rather than working and growing through their mistakes, many men chose to blame the woman for all that goes wrong in marriage—only to discover there is no such thing as a conflict- or challenge-free marriage. (As I said earlier, even Adam blamed Eve for the fall of man.)

Our sons need to be taught while they are young what love in action looks like from a woman's perspective. All these things will teach our sons that marriage is not perfect, that prayer and repentance are the way to restoring peace in the home, and most important, that God can and does help us love and forgive each other no matter how much we disagree.

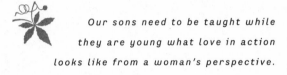

*Our sons need to be taught while they are young what love in action looks like from a woman's perspective.*

My son Jake is now eighteen, and my training time with him is coming to a close. But already I see the fruits of my labor in Jake's transparency. He has learned to take responsibility for his actions, he is quick to reconcile, and he knows that when conflict comes it is time to pray.

*For we are not fighting against people made of flesh and blood, but against the evil rulers and authorities of the unseen world, against those mighty powers of darkness who rule this world, and against wicked spirits in the heavenly realms.*

Ephesians 6:12, NLT

## A Mother's Prayer

Dear God,
Put a love in my son's heart
for his future wife that is so strong
he will do whatever it takes to fight for
his marriage, not against it.
Open his eyes to the spiritual attacks
that will come. Help him face his
relational challenges head-on in
Your strength, not his own.
Give me the wisdom I need to
raise a tender warrior for Your kingdom.
Thank You that I am not alone in my labors.
In Your name I pray, amen.

# chapter six

# Teach Him to Honor and Respect a Woman

*Daughters of kings are here,*
*and your bride stands at your right side,*
*wearing a wedding gown trimmed with pure gold.*

PSALM 45:9, CEV

One of the greatest challenges of teaching boys how to honor and respect women is that many girls today are not being raised to act like daughters of the King. Countless young women behave as though they are unworthy of respect—from themselves or others. This disrespect is often reflected in the way men treat woman today.

We have allowed modern-day television shows, movies, and advertising to blind our daughters and sons to their God-given roles and to strip them of their modesty. They are learning to take advantage of each other's weaknesses rather than honor and respect one another. Due to this, our boys view women as sexual objects rather than people of honor. More and more, girls find their worth in their sexuality.

Rather than becoming the woman she wants to be, today's young woman is starved for affection, walking around dressed half naked, and giving herself sexually to any man who will make her believe (for a night) that he loves her. Although many men will take advantage of a woman like this, deep down they resent her for allowing them to disrespect her—much like a son resents his mother for not disciplining him or setting boundaries. The truth of the matter is that no matter how a man acts toward a woman, deep down he desires a lady who commands his respect.

As mothers, we can put a stop to the negative cycle by teaching our sons to become gentlemen who honor and respect women the way God intended from the beginning.

## Life Happens

If you watch for teachable moments, life will become less frustrating when unplanned events happen. Take for example, the following story.

My friend Chris has three sons and a daughter, and she utilizes every opportunity to teach her boys about honoring and caring for women. She teaches them to open the door for her, has them bring in her groceries, and shows them by example what a real lady acts like. Chris is doing a great job of training those boys to assume their rightful positions as men.

One day Chris and her children were shopping at Costco when all of a sudden a teaching opportunity presented itself. Her daughter, Emma, felt sick to her stomach and threw up all over herself. At that moment Chris had a choice: She could either buy Emma a new outfit, or she could ask one of her sons to volunteer his shirt so his sister could walk out of the store modestly covered.

As it turned out, all three of her boys were willing to give up their shirts for their sister. They also learned a valuable lesson that day: A real man honors a woman—in this case, their sister—by sacrificing his own comfort when necessary.

If my dear friend had bought her daughter new clothing, not only would she have gone over her family's monthly budget, but she would also have missed an opportunity to teach her sons about honoring and caring for someone they love.

## A Mother's Influence

You are the woman in your son's life for now, and you need to model for him what a lady acts like. It is your privilege and responsibility to train him to respond like a gentleman in every situation.

As we discussed earlier, it is much easier to train a boy than change a man. You can shape and mold your beloved boy while he is still young, whether you have a good male role model in your home or not. You can teach him to treat you with honor and respect.

*It is much easier to train a boy than change a man.*

Whether he is a toddler or a teen, your son should treat you like a lady. Teach him now that sometimes it is necessary to sacrifice his own comfort for yours in order to treat you like a princess. Your son can set a new standard for his generation to follow!

## A Mother in Action

### Ages 3–8
At this stage in your boy's life, you are his world. Take advantage of this teachable time by training him to act like a gentleman who respects and honors women.

1. **Teach him to speak kindly to others.** Do not let him boss you around or talk down to you. If he does, remind him that you are his mother; if he does not honor you with his words, he will be punished. The danger of letting him disrespect you, even in jest, is that he will grow

up thinking it is acceptable to show disrespect to other women, including his wife.

2. **Have him open doors for you.** It may be difficult to let your baby act as your doorman, but your son needs to learn creative ways to honor women. So when you are going out any door, ask him to open it for you—then be sure to thank him.

3. **Reward him with praise.** Praise is a powerful motivator and an excellent teaching device. When your son displays good manners and shows respect toward others, make a big deal of it. Both boys and grown men feel loved when a woman expresses verbal appreciation of them.

## Ages 9–13
Continue the above and add the following:

1. **Explain about the life advantages.** At this age your son may start questioning why he has to do what you ask and what the point of it all is. This is a great time to let him know about the advantages that come with acting like a gentleman (e.g., success, respect, and a good wife).

2. **Point out both negative and positive male role models.** Most boys are visual learners. Help your son learn to recognize the difference between good and bad male role models by pointing them out in movies, on television shows, and in real life.

   For example, the next time a man lets you go first or

opens the door for you, thank him in front of your son. Then take a moment to explain to your son why that gesture was honoring to you.

On the other hand, when you see a man acting like an idiot to a woman, do not ignore the situation or act as if it were okay. Rather, tell your son it is not right to talk that way or act like that to a woman—*ever*. Win the battle in your boy's mind by teaching him to distinguish right actions and attitudes from wrong.

3.  **Never, ever let him mistreat you.** It is your God-given responsibility as a mother to be the one woman in your son's life who requires honor and respect from him. You will devastate your boy's relationship with his future wife if you let him mistreat you or speak disrespectfully to you.

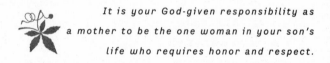

*It is your God-given responsibility as a mother to be the one woman in your son's life who requires honor and respect.*

I would venture to guess that many abusive men had mothers who allowed their sons and their sons' fathers to disrespect them and mistreat them. If you refuse to discipline your son for disrespectful actions toward you or any other woman, other people will suffer—including your future grandchildren.

4. **Make his friends respect your rules.** When your son's male friends are in your home, insist that they be respectful and well-mannered. Do not change your rules just because you have company. If you allow his friends to negatively influence the way you teach him, you will water down your work in his life and cause him to respect his friends more than his own mother.

   By being firm and consistent about enforcing the ground rules in your home, you are doing more than training your son to honor his mother; you are also teaching his friends the lost art of acting like a gentleman.

## Ages 14–19
Continue the above training and add the following:

1. **Train him to speak respectfully to others.** We live in an age where television shows and peers teach our sons that it is acceptable to use foul language or discuss inappropriate subjects (sex, porn) around girls. Teach your son how to redirect the conversation to more appropriate topics and to use respectful language in the presence of women or girls. Whether the girl acts like a true lady or not, your son can set the tone of the conversation.

2. **Greet him and his friends.** When your son or his friends come into your home, get up from what you are doing and welcome them warmly. By standing to acknowledge anyone who enters your home, you are showing your teen what it means to treat people with honor and respect.

3. **Set up date nights with your son.** Who better to teach your son how to act like a gentleman on a real date than you?

   While you are on the date together, do not ask him about his homework, his house chores, or any other "nagging mother" topics. Rather, have fun! Let him select the restaurant, and encourage him to practice considerate gestures like opening your door, pulling out your chair, ordering for you, and paying with his own money. If he is old enough, let him drive.

   During the meal, prompt him to ask you questions about your day and to steer the conversation toward things that are of mutual interest to you both. This will teach him to explore conversational topics outside his comfort zone, which will benefit him when he is courting his future wife.

4. **Ask him to help at mealtime.** Teach him how to set the table (including the proper order for place settings), sit and behave during dinner, clear dishes, and properly clean up the kitchen after a meal—right down to refrigerating leftovers and wiping down countertops.

Make a big deal of it when he helps you without being asked—tell him how wonderful he is and what a great husband he will be someday. Remind him what a rare treasure it is for a woman to find a true gentleman, and that this is an important area of gentlemanliness.

5. **Assume the best of him.** Whenever your son makes plans to spend time at a friends' house, particularly a girl's house, let him know that you trust him and will be praying for him. Remember, affirming your son and giving him the opportunity to be a gentleman is far more motivating than assuming the worst and treating him accordingly.

## The Big Picture

When I was a teen, my dad sat me down one day and said, "Watch how any boy you date treats his mother; that is how he will treat his wife someday."

*"Watch how any boy you date treats his mother; that is how he will treat his wife someday."*

I found these wise words to be of great help when I was searching for a husband. Shortly after Steve and I got engaged, I was invited to his family reunion. I knew this would be my last chance to observe Steve before I said "I do," and I did so carefully. I was relieved to see that he treated his mother and two sisters with great honor and respect. He opened doors for them and jumped up to help carry in groceries; he was polite and well mannered.

We have now been married for nineteen years, and he still treats me with the same excellent manners and respect as when we were dating. I often thank my in-laws for how they raised their son.

I encourage you to teach your son to honor and respect all women. He and your daughter-in-law will one day thank you for your efforts.

*Show proper respect to everyone.*
*Love the community of believers.*
*Have respect for God. Honor the king.*

1 PETER 2:17, NIRV

## A Mother's Prayer for Understanding

☙

Dear God,

Help me to show my son what it

means to honor and respect women.

Protect him from the world's influence,

grow him into a well-respected leader,

and show him how to treat a lady.

Let his actions reflect that he is Yours.

Give me the influence I need in his life

to teach him, Lord, and may he also

learn from the godly male role

models You place in his life.

In Your name I pray, amen.

# chapter seven

# Teach Him to Be a Man
# of His Word

*Simply let your 'Yes' be 'Yes,' and your
'No,' 'No'; anything beyond this comes from the evil one.*

MATTHEW 5:37, NIV

*O*ur boys are being trained to
say whatever they need to in order to get what they want—
in other words, to lie without conscience or consequence.
Too many modern-day politicians, celebrities, and yes, even
fathers have led our sons to believe that broken promises are
acceptable so long as the end result makes them happy.

Our heavenly Father warns us that when we do not keep
our word, evil things happen. If that sounds a little dramatic
on our Creator's part, just take a look at the damage wreaked
by the broken families strewn across this continent, in many
cases because men have not been taught to keep their word.

We have a crisis on our hands and it must be dealt with immediately. We are responsible for teaching our beloved boys to discern truth from lies and to keep their promises. We can establish a new generation of men by training our boys to become men of their word.

*We can establish a new generation of men by training our boys to become men of their word.*

## Life Happens

As a conference speaker, I have enjoyed being a guest in some of the most gorgeous homes in the country.

I will never forget one situation in particular. I had been asked to speak at a ladies' luncheon being held at a sprawling estate. Steve, Jacob, and I were coming straight from our church's family camp—so we had our travel trailer hitched to the back of our vehicle.

We arrived in the early evening at our hosts' gorgeous hacienda, which boasted breathtaking mountain views and horses roaming the countryside. As we enjoyed the delicious dinner her cook had prepared, our hostess looked out the window, saw our tent trailer, and exclaimed, "Oh, you brought your tent. We weren't sure what we were going to do with you, because we really aren't comfortable letting strangers sleep in our home."

*Imagine having a mansion with seventeen bedrooms in the middle of nowhere,* I thought, *and insisting your invited guests sleep outside in the cold of winter!* But I responded lightly, "Yeah, no problem! We can sleep on the lawn outside."

She said, "Oh, good!"—and sounded, I thought, a little too relieved.

I shot a furtive glance at Steve. We were beginning to get the picture.

It was getting toward bedtime, but we were still at the table finishing our dessert when our hostess said cheerily, "Are you all ready to go out and go to bed in your tent? I'd like to go ahead and lock up the house."

I didn't want to make a bad impression in front of four-year-old Jacob, so I said, "Sure, that's fine!"

At that moment Jacob innocently asked, "Mommy, why are we sleeping outside? It's cold out there, and I'm scared!"

Fighting my impulse to say, *Because this paranoid, stingy woman won't let us sleep in one of her bazillion bedrooms,* I told him instead, "Just think—we can go to sleep looking at the beautiful stars! We'll get to sleep by the animals and have a campout."

Moments later, as we made our way into the chilly night, the door locked solidly behind us.

The next morning I was wondering whether we'd have to wash up in the horse trough when our hostess appeared at our campsite and said, "I wanted to invite you inside to shower and get ready for the luncheon."

I followed her inside, controlling my desire to suggest professional counseling. As I got ready, I found myself thinking, *Why should I speak at this ladies' luncheon after this woman has treated me and my family like hired help with the measles?*

Just then, Jake came into the bathroom and began to cry. "Why are we here, Mommy? I want to go home!"

I felt the same way, but I immediately recognized an opportunity to teach him about the importance of keeping one's word—even when we feel like others don't deserve it. In that moment, my resentment turned into determination to make the best of an awkward situation.

God proved His purpose that day. After I spoke, a very sad, broken mother and her teenage sons approached me. Tears of joy were running down this woman's cheeks, and her sons were hugging and loving on their mom like little boys on Christmas morning. They told me their mother hadn't spoken a word in two years because their dad had abused them and then run off with another woman. She and her boys needed some hope and a new start. On that very day, she said, she had found the strength to forgive her ex-husband and finish strong in raising her sons.

At that moment I did not care if my family and I had to sleep in a pigpen. I was so excited to share with Jake why God had sent us there—and why the devil tried to get us to go home before we did the work of the Lord!

## A Mother's Influence

It is hard to keep our word when we are disappointed in someone or something. But in order to teach our sons to become men of their word, we first have to be women of our word. This means being careful about what you commit to or the promises you make, especially to your son.

*In order to teach our sons to become men of their word, we first have to be women of our word.*

## A Mother in Action

*Ages 3–8*

1. **Hold a hard line.** It's easy to wimp out rather than make your little boy keep his word, especially when he bats his eyelashes at you and cries a little. However, you need to teach him to become a man of his word. If you are not firm with him about following through on commitments, he will not grasp the importance of keeping his promises. And believe me, it will become increasingly harder to train him about this when he gets into his preteen years.

2. **Start with the little things.** If your son tells you he'll clean his room or take out the trash, then claims he is too busy or tired, do not let him out of his commitment. If he promises to attend someone's birthday party but on the day of the party no longer feels like going, don't let him skip out.

3. **Make him keep his promises.** Teach him now that the only acceptable reasons for breaking a promise are an emergency or illness. If your son wants to try a new sport, make sure he is committed to giving it his all—because you will not allow him to quit, even if he ends up not liking the sport or the coach.

    By starting this policy at a young age, you are teaching him how important it is to think through decisions and weigh consequences before making a commitment. You are teaching him, in essence, how important it is to keep his word.

*Ages 9–13*
Continue all the above and add the following:

1. **Work out a schedule.** One of the best ways to keep your son from overcommitting himself is to sit down and discuss the balance between his schedule and his family responsibilities. Teach him that it is just as important to keep his word to you, his mother, as it is to honor promises made to others.

2. **Stress the importance of commitment.** Once you have figured out together what he is going to commit to, tell him that should he back out, there will be consequences. Be serious and firm when addressing the importance of keeping his word.

3. **Set an example.** When you commit to doing something for or with him, do whatever it takes to keep your word. *Nothing* will hinder your influence in his life more than a string of broken promises. On the other hand, if you live it, you can demand the same of your son—and because of your example, he'll respond positively.

## Ages 14–19

There's no doubt about it: The teen years are when the rubber meets the road. Everything you have taught your son up to this point will now have to be lived out in front of him. Your teen no longer does what you say; he does what you do. This is your final season with your son, and it is more important than ever that you finish strong.

Continue all the above and add the following:

1. **Do not let him run his own life yet.** No matter what he says to you, he is not ready for that kind of freedom. He still lives under your roof, and he must obey your rules. Don't let his curfew slide or his family chores and school responsibilities be pushed aside. If you do, you're setting your son up for failure regarding rules and responsibilities.

2. **Remind him.** Encourage him to remember that his word is his credibility. When someone breaks a promise to him, gently turn it into a teaching lesson on why he shouldn't break his word to others.

3. **Choose your words carefully.** Be careful how you speak to him when he does let you down—you can inflict damage by criticizing him harshly. For example, if he tells you that no one else keeps their promises, remind him that he is better than that, and that he has way too much going for him to be a flake. Or start out by saying, "I know you want to be a man of your word—and I want to help you."

4. **Be his cheerleader.** He needs to know up front that you are on his team and that you're strict with him only because you want the best for his life. So remind him of that fact often—it will work wonders in how he perceives your guiding role in his life.

## The Big Picture

Nothing makes a wife feel more secure than knowing she can trust her husband to keep his promises.

*Nothing makes a wife feel more secure than knowing she can trust her husband to keep his promises.*

Although my parents are divorced, one thing I know for certain about my dad is that he would rather die than break a promise to me. His mother, my Jewish grandmother, raised her son to be a man of his word at all costs. She knew that his word was his bond and the key to his success in life. And it's true: People tell me all the time that they trust my dad to do whatever he commits to.

We live in an era where too many potentially great men have lost sight of the power of a promise. However, women still long for—and hold in the highest regard—a man of his word.

> *God is not a man, that he should lie.*
> *He is not a human, that he should change his mind.*
> *Has he ever spoken and failed to act?*
> *Has he ever promised and not carried it through?*
>
> NUMBERS 23:19, NLT

## A Mother's Prayer

∽

Dear heavenly Father,

I lift my son, Your child, up before You.

Please help him become man of his word.

Give him discernment to know truth

from lies and the will to do what is right.

Let him learn to trust Your Word and

deposit its truth in his heart and mind.

Help me be strong in wisdom and discipline

while I am raising him. Let him experience

firsthand the rewards of keeping his word.

In Your name I pray, amen.

# chapter eight

# Teach Him the Power of Purity

*The thief's purpose is to steal and kill and destroy.*
*My purpose is to give life in all its fullness.*

JOHN 10:10, NLT

*T*he devil does not have to defeat us to steal our boys. All he has to do is distract us from protecting our sons.

If a police officer came to your door and warned you that your neighbor's boys had just been mugged and then murdered, you would be on the lookout for anything that might let that enemy in your home or near your loved ones.

God warns in His Word that there is an enemy after us, and he is out to steal, kill, and destroy us and our boys. If we are not careful, we will aid him in his mission. This is too often accomplished through what we allow our sons to read, watch, and listen to.

*The devil does not have to defeat us to steal our boys. All he has to do is distract us from protecting our sons.*

The devil uses many venues to destroy boys' minds, morals, and manhood. The more mindless entertainment they take in, the less capable they are of distinguishing right from wrong and good from evil.

Can you imagine sending soldiers into battle unarmed? They would be the laughingstock of the military and decimated by their enemies.

Our homes need to be places of refuge where our sons can find peace for their young minds, protection for their hearts, and training to prepare them for the mental and physical battles they will have to fight every time they exit our homes. Consider these years their training ground for the giants they will fight to protect their own families someday.

*If we really want victory for our beloved boys,
our lives will have to be louder
than the world's influence.*

## Life Happens

I have a husband, a teenage son, and a six-year-old daughter, and I'm really protective about what I allow into our home. As a result, people often look at me funny when I tell them we don't have cable television.

It occurred to me one day that if I paid forty dollars a month to receive several hundred channels, I would be opening the door of our home to the enemy. I would essentially be inviting him in so that he could attack and undermine the godly values and character I'm trying to instill in my children. I would be paying for my son and daughter to learn how to disrespect a parent through cartoons and sitcoms that portray parents as complete idiots and show children running the household.

As if all that isn't dangerous and damaging enough, my son and husband would be exposed to countless images of sex, women, and violence as they flipped through the bazillion channels I allowed in my home. Boys struggle enough as it is with lust and conflicting messages in society; why would I want to pay to push my son into the pit of impurity?

We have only a very short time with our sons, and in the busyness of life we need to grab what we can. Ask yourself, *Will hours spent watching television help prepare my son to be a husband? Or is it going to teach him to tune out his future family and confuse him about who and what a real man is supposed to be?*

## A Mother's Influence

It is your privilege and responsibility to train your son, while he is in your home and under your influence, to be a godly husband who knows how to fight battles of the mind. If you let television or his friends dictate his moral code, you are setting him up to fall into the trap of temptation. If, however, you make your home a place of purity and refuge, then your son will be able to discern right from wrong and love from lust.

*If you let television or his friends dictate his moral code, you are setting him up to fall into the trap of temptation.*

# A Mother in Action

*Ages 3–8*

1. **Purify your home.** You are probably thinking, *My son is little; I don't need to deal with the issue of purity now.* You may not need to talk about sex with three-to-eight-year-olds, but it is never too early to begin setting up your home as a place of purity. You can do a great deal to protect his little eyes from seeing sexual images by carefully monitoring the movies you watch at home or the magazines and catalogs you receive (for example, Victoria's Secret).

2. **Be honest.** Whether it be on television or in a movie, if your little one happens to catch a glance of a sexual relationship happening outside of marriage, make a point of telling him that mommies and daddies should not sleep in the same bed until they are married.

3. **Cover up.** When getting dressed or showering, try not to walk around naked in front of your little boy. Let him know that private body parts should stay covered. It is good to instill modesty in your son at an early age, before he finds himself struggling with the issue of purity.

*Ages 9–13*
Continue all the above and add the following:

1. **Be careful where you let him go.** By this age, if your son has gone home with friends whose mothers do not protect their homes, most likely he has seen a grown woman naked—either in a magazine or on the Internet. Do not be afraid to ask your son about the kind of atmosphere he'll encounter when he visits his friends' homes.

2. **Talk to him openly.** Remind him to always guard his mind—not in an embarrassing way, but in a way he can relate to. For example: "Honey, your friends' parents probably don't live exactly the way we do, so remember to be on your guard and not give in to any temptations to look at or do things that will hurt you later."

3. **Be cautious about sleepovers.** One rule we established in our home from the time Jake was little is never to let him stay overnight at friends' houses, even if we know the family. I set this rule after speaking to many youth groups and discovering that almost all acts of sin happen when spending the night at friends' homes—even good Christian homes. However, I encourage Jake to invite any of his friends to sleep over at our home, where I can control the environment around him.

Be wise about where you let your son wander; he will go as far as you allow.

*Ages 14–19*
Continue all the above and add the following:

1.  **Talk to him like an adult.** A mother does not have to turn into an old-fashioned prude in order to instill purity in her teenage son. At this age you can talk to your son more like an adult. "Because I said so" or "Christians don't watch that kind of stuff" makes God out to be no fun, rather than a loving father who wants the best in life for all His children.

2.  **Do not assume your son does not struggle.** I have discovered something from hundreds of conversations with teen boys while speaking at churches around the country. When parents pretend their boys do not struggle or avoid the issue of sexual purity altogether, boys naturally become either more curious or more rebellious. On the other hand, when boys feel safe sharing with their parents about their struggles, a lot of the temptation to experience sin is removed. Keep in mind that a man's greatest battle is dealing with sexual purity, so it is important that you help him fight the temptation rather than being drawn to it.

3.  **Pray for his purity.** Sexual temptation for your son is just as much a spiritual battle as it is a physical battle, so cover him in prayer for purity every day. Better yet, pray with him for a pure heart and protection from temptation.

*Sexual temptation for your son is just as much a spiritual battle as it is a physical battle.*

4. **Continue to make your home a place of purity.** Do not open the door to temptation (e.g., unmonitored Internet access, cable television, and women's fashion magazines and catalogs). Your son struggles enough outside your home; he needs a place of rest and a refuge from the battles he fights every day in his mind.

5. **Encourage wholesome entertainment in your home.** Above all, make sure your son and his friends feel welcome in your home. I actually prayed that God would provide a Ping-Pong table for our garage and a pool table in our living room. And you know what? God answered. I keep lots of good, healthy snack food accessible because my son and his friends seem to have bottomless pits for stomachs. We host a pizza night every week in our home. (What teen can resist free pizza?)

   On Christmas and Valentine's Day, I hold a cookie-decorating contest for my son and his friends. It is amazing what happens when you remove the pressure to "be cool" and give them a chance to be creative.

   Another innovative way to connect with your teen is to challenge him and his friends to a card or board game.

This kind of friendly competition is a great way to converse face-to-face with your son and his friends.

6. **Encourage open communication.** Reassure your son that it is natural to struggle with sexual purity, and that he can conquer it and remain pure. Foster an atmosphere in which he feels comfortable talking to you about anything regarding sex—or he will go elsewhere to find his answers. Do not judge or criticize him in your efforts to help him stay pure.

7. **Paint a picture of his wife.** Remind him of his wedding day and how special his wife will feel if she is the only one he has sex with. Pray with him for his wife so he will seal in his mind a picture of that great day.

## The Big Picture

The big picture is so obvious on this topic. Just think about all the great men that have traded success, ministry, and marriage for a moment's pleasure. What if these men had been trained from the time they were little boys to protect themselves from the enemy's trap?

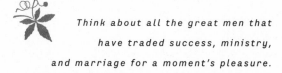

*Think about all the great men that have traded success, ministry, and marriage for a moment's pleasure.*

Many fallen men live with regret and wish they could reverse the damage done by their sin. Our sons can help reestablish the moral fiber in this great nation; they can become faithful husbands in a fallen world. Let's do our part as mothers by training them to run the race and finish strong.

*But remember that the temptations that come into your life are no different from what others experience. And God is faithful. He will keep the temptation from becoming so strong that you can't stand up against it. When you are tempted, he will show you a way out so that you will not give in to it.*

1 CORINTHIANS 10:13, NLT

## A Mother's Prayer

Dear God,
I lift up my son to You. I ask You, Lord,
to guard his heart and mind.
Give him spiritual eyes to see the
enemy's traps. Protect him from
going places or seeing things that
will cause him to fall. Show me how to
set up my home as a refuge
for his mind and spirit.
In Your name I pray, amen.

# chapter nine

# Teach Him to Provide for His Family

*If anyone does not provide for his relatives,*
*and especially for his immediate family,*
*he has denied the faith and is worse*
*than an unbeliever.*

1 TIMOTHY 5:8, NIV

*M*en are called by God
Himself to provide for their households. However, our men
and boys are becoming less and less motivated to provide for
their family because they have watched the social trend of
woman learning to do it all.

Today's modern woman is smart, self-sufficient, and successful apart from a man. In many cases, wives make more
money than their husbands. Today, more women lead corpo-
rate America than ever before. When it comes to the

male/female roles in the workplace, it is a far cry from the way God designed things in the beginning.

In addition, millions of single moms act as sole provider and parent for their children. Now, I am not saying mothers should not work. I personally tasted the fruits of success and loved it before I had children. The thrill of accomplishing something great feels good to any woman. However, we must ask ourselves, *At what price does success come? What message are we independent, do-it-myself moms sending our beloved boys?*

*What message are we independent, do-it-myself moms sending our beloved boys?*

Something happens to women's hearts when their first child is born—God changes us whether we realize it or not! The joy of career fulfillment is diminished by the thrill of becoming a mother. Our children's welfare suddenly becomes more important than our career aspirations, and we crave their precious hugs and kisses more than the paycheck or the approval from a superior.

Deep down, most women long to be integrally involved in their children's lives. When a woman is forced to work because her husband cannot or will not provide for his family, she often begins to resent him for taking away her

God-given desire to call "motherhood" her main job.

I know many of you reading this right now are single moms or women whose husbands are unable to provide for you and your children. I want to share with you that I, too, work outside my home in order to help meet our financial needs. But the greater picture here is that God knows our hearts. He knows that we long to be provided for; it is part of His perfect will for women. Unfortunately, we live in an imperfect world. We strive to achieve the balance between a need to work and a yearning to be tuned in to our homes.

Take comfort in knowing that your Father in heaven will care for and protect your children when you cannot be there.

## Life Happens

When my dad was just thirteen years old, his father suffered a major heart attack and could no longer work. At that young age, my dad was forced to become the sole provider for his family.

Before my grandpa passed away, he drilled it into my dad that he was the man of the house and that a real man takes care of his family. Needless to say, my dad learned at a young age about real-life responsibility. As heartbreaking as it was for him to see his father ill and to be forced to provide for his family, he received something of far more worth than an easy childhood with no challenges, something that is sadly missing in our young men today: an understanding of what it means to be "the man of the house." He also learned the self-discipline he would need to become the successful man he is today.

Many times life's heartbreaks and disappointments produce great men of our beloved boys. My dad is a great provider who would go without in order to make sure his family is taken care of.

When he was just nineteen, he met and married my mom, and he worked three jobs to make ends meet. He always told me while I was growing up that his greatest joy in life was taking care of me. His mother was a smart woman for not taking the pressure off him when times got tough for their finances and family.

## A Mother's Influence

If your husband provides for your family, make a point of telling him in front of your son how much you appreciate him. If you are not provided for, use the situation for divine training by telling your son the truth. Tell him that it is not God's will for all the financial responsibility to fall on the woman. Let him know that, deep down, every woman desires to be taken care of and provided for by the man she loves.

*It is not God's will for all the financial responsibility to fall on the woman.*

It is important that you set an example of trusting in the Lord to meet your needs. But be careful not to make it look so easy that your boy grows up believing it is okay to let the woman carry the financial burden. Teach your son now that God's perfect picture of marriage is for a husband to work hard to provide for his wife and kids.

Remember, your son loves you. And if he understands how difficult this is for you, despite the fact that you maintain a good attitude and a joyful spirit, he will want to do whatever it takes to keep from putting this kind of financial pressure on his own wife when he grows up.

## A Mother in Action

### Ages 3–8

1. **Be creative.** Think up some fun, creative ways to start your young son on the road to becoming a great provider. For example, when he wants to buy a toy, allow him to earn the money for it by helping out around the house. For a friend's birthday present or at Christmastime, encourage him to think up creative ways to earn money, like opening a lemonade stand or making cookies or a simple, handcrafted ornament to sell.

2. **Teach him about tithing.** Pay him for his chores, then teach him to give 10 percent of his earnings to God. Have him designate a separate piggy bank for tithing.

Nothing will secure his financial future more than teaching him the law of giving.

3. **Let him buy his own treats.** When you're at the grocery store and he wants something that's not on your grocery list, allow him to purchase it out of his allowance. In other words, do *not* give your son everything he wants—if you do, you will weaken his desire to provide for a family someday. We have all seen the rotten fruit that comes of a spoiled mama's boy.

*Ages 9–13*

Continue the above and add the following:

1. **Open a savings account.** This is a great age to teach him about finances. Have him open his own bank account so he can learn to save and manage money. Encourage him to deposit a designated portion of everything he receives—birthday money, lawn-mowing money, etc. Encourage him to look carefully at the monthly statements, and talk about different ways for him to earn more money.

2. **Teach him about ongoing expenses.** If he wants his own cell phone, have him do enough chores around the house to earn his portion of the monthly bill. Paying his own share of a cell phone bill every month can help teach him about long-term financial commitment.

3. **Let him treat you.** If he wants to go out to the movies with you, occasionally let him pay your way with his own money. At a restaurant, let him help with the tip—which will serve the dual purpose of teaching him how much is appropriate and honing his math skills (15 to 20 percent of the total is standard for excellent service and food).

4. **Offer to match funds.** If he wants to purchase an expensive item, challenge him to save up for it. An excellent incentive might be offering to match his funds up to a certain limit. Saving for something over a long period of time will teach him a valuable lesson about delayed gratification, which will in turn improve his ability to think through situations and make wise decisions.

*Ages 14–19*
Continue the above and add the following:

1. **Encourage him to seek employment.** By the time he is fifteen, encourage him to look for a part-time job after school, on weekends, or during the summer.

   Now, I know many parents do not think their teens should have to work; their reasoning generally falls somewhere along the lines of "Childhood is so short anyway; he'll be in the workforce for the rest of his life." My feeling about this is that if your son is busy working, he is learning multiple responsibilities: committing to a job, budgeting his time, and making his own money. He will also be less likely to get into trouble if he is at a job during his free time.

2. **Teach him to be responsible.** You will help him become financially responsible by letting him pay for his own cell phone or buy his own clothes. Encourage him to write his own checks, make his own deposits, and budget his own money.

3. **Let him pay.** Always require that your son repay you for money he borrows or fill up your car with gas when he borrows it. When you take him clothes shopping, give him the predetermined amount so he will learn to spend wisely. If you give him free rein to buy whatever he wants, he will not learn to manage money.

4. **Talk about different career options.** Men are at their happiest when they love what they do for a living. Start by looking for your son's natural gifting and observing what makes him come alive; then encourage him to explore professions related to those interests.

   For example, if he loves animals, he could volunteer at the humane society or talk to a local veterinarian about the field of animal science. If he is good at math, have him explore a career in accounting. If he enjoys debating and is a logical thinker, encourage him to consider becoming a lawyer. Our son is a great writer, and I talk to him often about becoming a published author. However, authors rarely make enough money to take care of a family, so I also talk to him about his amazing social skills and how good he would be in the field of sales.

## The Big Picture

Our sons will become good providers if they are taught that it is the manly thing to do, as well as God's recipe for a healthy marriage.

Remember, deep down every man wants to rescue a woman. Don't kill that desire to provide by pretending all is perfect with or without a man.

Your son represents the next generation of men. Raising him to believe it is acceptable for a woman to financially support the family will hinder his desire to provide for his own wife and family someday. On the other hand, helping him understand his position as provider will bless him greatly. It will also ensure the future success of his career and marriage.

> *Our people have to learn to be diligent*
> *in their work so that all necessities are met*
> *(especially among the needy) and they don't*
> *end up with nothing to show for their lives.*
> TITUS 3:14, *THE MESSAGE*

*A Mother's Prayer*

⌀

Dear God,

I pray You would help my son find

his gift and give him the desire

to become a man who provides well

for his future family. Order his steps

toward success according to

Your perfect will, and give him

favor with You and with man.

In Your name I pray, amen.

# chapter ten

# Teach Him to Have a Real Relationship with God

*I pour out my complaints before him*
*and tell him all my troubles.*
*For I am overwhelmed, and you*
*alone know the way I should turn.*

PSALM 142:2–3, NLT

ead any of the psalms and it becomes obvious that there was nothing artificial about King David's relationship with God. David didn't hide his anger, his fears, his disappointments, his worries, his failure, his praise, his needs, his dreams, or his love from his heavenly Father. He did not care what others thought when it came to his love for his Daddy in heaven.

Because of this kind of relationship, David got to experience God's grace, God's power, God's favor, God's blessing, and yes, even God's forgiveness—when he fell into sin with Bathsheba. He is called the man after God's own heart even though he was far from perfect. David knew how to have a real love relationship with his Lord.

I have traveled throughout the country and spoken to thousands of young people from good Christian homes who only know God by name, like some distant relative they have never met. They know the dos and don'ts of Christianity, they know guilt, they know obligation, and yes, they know their Bible verses. They know hypocrisy and how to put on a show for their parents. But sadly, they do not know God as their heavenly Father.

Maybe it's because they have never really had a personal encounter with God. Maybe parents put too much pressure on their sons to be perfect Christians so they can look like perfect parents. My guess is that many parents care more about looking spiritual than about developing a real relationship with God.

*Maybe parents put too much pressure on their sons to be perfect Christians so they can look like perfect parents.*

Going to a church building or putting on a show for others will not do anything to bring us or our sons closer to God. This is a generation of boys that will not tolerate or accept man-made rules or religion. They want what is real. Why do you think the reality shows have become more popular than the scripted Hollywood productions? It is because humans are drawn to reality. It's time to teach our sons and ourselves, through King David's example, how to "get real" with God.

If our sons are going to become great husbands and mighty warriors for their King, they need to see God in action. They need to witness His power in their prayers, understand their place in His eternal plan, and most important, know Him as their Father in heaven.

> *If our sons are going to become great husbands and mighty warriors for their King, they need to see God in action.*

## Life Happens

Several years ago Steve and I went to Seattle to produce a showcase for models, actors, and singers. After auditioning more than three thousand applicants, we selected 150 individuals to participate in the production.

The day after the audition, while we were preparing to begin rehearsals for the show, a scuffle in the lobby caught my attention: A couple of grubby teenagers were causing a scene, and it was apparent they were about to be booted out onto the street by the security guard.

*These boys can't possibly be part of our show,* I thought as I approached them cautiously.

No sooner had I thought that when two of the boys called out to me. I gulped. Obviously, they were two of the three thousand who had auditioned but didn't make the cut. This was all I needed—gang members causing problems for our crew and all our young performers!

I watched the security guard escort them out and whispered a quick prayer of thanks. As I prayed, God grabbed my attention with this verse: "Man looks at the outward appearance, but the LORD looks at the heart" (1 Samuel 16:7, NIV).

My first thought was that nobody would ever make it in Hollywood following that verse! But then again, this showcase was meant to get people to heaven, not Hollywood.

I knew then what I had to do. God wanted me to invite those two gang members to spend the week working with us on our showcase. I quickly walked back through the lobby and outside.

As if on cue, the two boys turned and faced me. I was terrified. I glanced around, hoping to see the security guard. Since he was nowhere to be found, I got a death grip on my clipboard, folded my arms across my chest, and stepped forward, thinking, *I'm either hearing from God now, or I'm going to meet Him tonight.*

"I know you auditioned for the showcase," I began. "Rehearsal is starting. You both better get in there."

It took a moment for my words to sink in.

"Forget it, Barbie!" one of them sneered. "We weren't picked, 'cause we don't got no talent."

"And no money," added the second.

"Well, I think you'll do great in this showcase," I replied, "and I should know. I'm the director. As far as money goes, your entry fee has been taken care of. So what do you say?"

They turned and peered at each other through their long, scraggly hair. "Cool!" they finally blurted, throwing their cigarettes down and following me inside.

I wasn't quite sure which category to put them in. Modeling? Acting? How about a new category for body odor? When we got to the room, the rehearsal was just about to begin. I introduced my new buddies to the staff, and we went on with business as usual.

That night, Steve, Jake, and I began to pray that these boys would find their real Father, the God who gave them life. We decided as a family to treat them as if they were our own sons. Every day I brought them lunch, just like I did for my son. Steve greeted them with hugs and told them how happy we were that they were spending the day with us.

By the third day they'd decided to take showers (praise God!). On the fourth day, one of the boys could hardly wait to tell me he hadn't smoked any pot the night before; the other proudly announced he'd given up smoking.

At the final dress rehearsal, when I shared my testimony and Steve shared the message of salvation, those two boys were the very first to come forward and give their lives to Jesus Christ. At the end of the altar call, they approached Steve and me and asked, "Could you be our spiritual parents?"

One of the boys continued, "When we were six and seven years old, our parents pushed us out of a car while they were driving through downtown Seattle, and we've never seen them again." He explained that ever since, they had been bounced around in the foster care system from one home to another. "Right now we're hiding out, and we're afraid."

All their lives, these boys had been told how bad they were. Every Christian they'd met was quick to say, "Look at all the poor choices you've made!" But now they knew their real heavenly Father, the God who gave them life.

All they needed was someone to introduce them to a real relationship with God. This wonderful work of God was just as much of a blessing for our son to witness as it was for those boys.

There is a big difference between teaching kids about God and connecting them to Him. I think many children who know about God still feel like an outsider, just like those boys. Maybe it's time to introduce our sons to a new kind of relationship with the Father—one that involves Him in their personal lives.

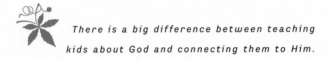

*There is a big difference between teaching kids about God and connecting them to Him.*

## A Mother's Influence

My greatest fear for Jake when he was born into our Christian family was that he would grow up to be a Revelation 3:16 Christian (lukewarm) and take God for granted. My fear was based on conversations I'd had at church camps with thousands of kids who never experienced God the way I did when I was saved at age twenty-four.

One thing I did to stop this from happening in Jake's heart was to pray with him for divine appointments so he could see God using him firsthand.

Proverbs 14:12 warns us that we do a lot of things that seem right to us, but that in the end lead to destruction. How sad would it be if you spent all your life preparing your son to become a godly husband and leader, only to find that he wants nothing to do with God when he grows up?

Let's do our part to raise a generation of boys who love the Lord with their whole heart, who know Him not only as God, but as their Father in heaven!

# A Mother in Action

*Ages 3–8*

1. **Encourage his childlike faith.** This is the best time to help your son get real with God—while he still has that childlike faith our heavenly Father desires in all of us. Take advantage of every opportunity to show your son how to be real with God. When he is crying, have him tell his Daddy in heaven what hurts. When he is happy or excited, lead him in thanking God for His goodness.

2. **Teach him to pray.** When he really wants something, have him pray that God would either grant it or change his heart. When he is angry, tell him how hard it is to process anger without God; then have him tell God in prayer why he is angry.

3. **Use biblical examples.** When he is getting ready to fall asleep, find out what he is thinking about. Then search out and read to him a Bible story that relates to the moment.

4. **Don't put on a show.** Let him know God wants our *hearts*. Never put pressure on him to perform his religion, like the Pharisees did back in biblical times. Too often our efforts to impress people with how spiritual we are actually hinder our children from experiencing a real relationship with God.

*Ages 9–13*
Continue the above and add the following:

1. **Pray for the little things.** Prayer is the best way to draw close to God. Too many Christian families only pray over meals or at church. While those are good habits to cultivate, they alone will not get your son truly connected to God. You need to set an example of what it looks like to get personal with God through prayer in everything.

2. **Read the psalms.** If you want your son to learn how to get real with God, read the psalms with him. Remember, the Word is the most powerful teaching tool of all.

3. **Remember that he is not perfect.** Be careful not to put pressure on your son to be the "perfect Christian." This portrays God as some mean guy in the sky just looking for a chance to punish him. I have met too many Christian kids that do not think they can measure up to their parents' expectations—so they throw in the towel on God.

4. **Turn up the praise music.** Don't be one of those parents who think there is only one kind of appropriate worship music. Go to your Christian bookstore or a reputable website and buy the style of Christian music your son likes to listen to. If he owns an mp3 player, let him download a few Christian songs he likes.

Remember, the goal is the message you want to deposit in his heart, not the style of music you do or do not like. If you deny him access to his style of music or try to force him to listen to yours, he will grow up resenting Christian music. On the other hand, if you grant him the freedom to listen to the kind of Christian music he loves, then you're automatically taking a stand against music that will only poison his soul.

5. **Let him see how God fits in his world.** Remember, it is not about you; it is about drawing him closer to God. So do what it takes to increase his faith. The apostle Paul says we need to become all things to all men—in other words, you need to speak your son's language with the Lord's message of truth.

*You need to speak your son's language
with the Lord's message of truth.*

*Ages 14–19*
Continue the above and add the following:

1. **Start with repentance.** If, by the time your son is this age, you have never really shown him how to be real with

God, I suggest you start with repentance. Ask him to forgive you for anything you may have done to confuse him about faith or to distance him from knowing God in a personal way.

Repentance is God's eraser for starting fresh and the key to building a new foundation of faith. You will never go wrong teaching your son how to get right with God.

> *Repentance is God's eraser for starting fresh and the key to building a new foundation of faith.*

King David wrote a lot of repentance prayers. If your son is going to grow into a godly man, he needs to learn now that his heavenly Father is always there to pick him up when he falls down.

2. **Keep it real.** Teens want and need what's real, especially while they are trying so hard to figure out who they are and what they believe. They need us to live out real faith in front of them and to know they can tell God anything.

3. **Keep praying with him.** I once met a teen boy whose parents were both in ministry, yet who had never prayed with his parents or seen them pray together. This broke my heart. What a tragedy—to commit your whole life to

God but leave your children wandering, aimless and alone, in their faith.

4. **Do not depend on your youth pastors to raise your teens up.** Your church's youth pastors are not your son's parents. Their job is to help, not raise him for you; to help him grow in God, not replace your parent role.

*Your church's youth pastors are not your son's parents.*

5. **Don't criticize.** Be careful not to put down your pastor or any leadership in the church in front of your son. If you do, you will kill any influence those dedicated individuals have in his life.

    Too many Christians spend Sunday afternoons criticizing their churches rather than affirming them. Sadly, this condemnation turns their children into cynical Christians whose tendency is to judge before they love.

6. **Remind him to build his faith on God, not people.** It is imperative that you teach your son not to build his foundation of faith on people but to stand on God's firm foundation of faith. Remind him that no one is perfect, but God is. He needs to learn this while he is young or he will eventually be let down. Get him to see his walk

with God like a racehorse with blinders on. I always tell my son, "Just run your race. Do not look anywhere else but to God alone!"

7. **Help him learn from his mistakes.** When your son makes a mistake, be sure to extend him the same kind of grace that God gives us. This will help him learn from his mistakes rather than give up. Remember that failure, no matter how big, is never final with our God.

> *Remember that failure, no matter how big, is never final with our God.*

## The Big Picture

There is nothing more powerful or comforting in this unstable world than seeing a real man with real faith in a real relationship with God. Men of faith know their God up close and personal. These mighty men of God have the power inside them to win wars, save nations, set captives free, kill giants in the land, and defeat the devil in every way. This kind of man lives for God and not for self. He makes our world a safer and better place.

Our God is the same today as He was back in biblical times. The only difference between the mighty men we see in the Bible and our sons is that those men knew God in a very personal, very real way. As a result, they got to experience God's presence and power in their lives firsthand.

How desperately our world needs our beloved boys to become strong and mighty men of faith!

*Love the LORD your God with all your heart and with all your soul and with all your strength.*

DEUTERONOMY 6:5, NIV

# A Mother's Prayer

❧

Dear God,

Reveal Yourself to my beloved son.

Open his heart to the things of

the Spirit, and help me teach him

how to be real with You.

Forgive me if I have done anything

to hinder his walk with You.

I want him to know You as his Father

and his personal Lord. I pray he will

never depart from You, and that he

will love You with his entire mind and

all his heart and all that is within him.

In Your name I pray, amen.

# chapter eleven

# Teach Him to Become
# a Godly Leader

*Husbands, love your wives, just as Christ loved the church
and gave himself up for her to make her holy, cleansing her
by the washing with water through the word, and to present
her to himself as a radiant church, without stain or wrinkle
or any other blemish, but holy and blameless.*

EPHESIANS 5:25–27, NIV

*A*ccording to the Word, a man's
dual responsibilities as spiritual leader are 1) to be representative of Christ at home and 2) to present his wife to God as a
radiant Christian woman. However, many women have, out
of necessity, become stronger spiritual influences in their
homes than their husbands.

In her heart of hearts, every woman longs for a strong,
godly man to lead her, and every man desires to be a great
leader of his family. However, many men do not know how
to execute their God-given responsibility and have relinquished that position to their wives.

*Every woman longs for a strong,
godly man to lead her, and every man
desires to be a great leader of his family.*

Unfortunately, many of these men had mothers who held the husband's position in their homes when they were growing up. This may have been because the father was absent, because the father figure set a bad example for the son to follow, or because the father was not spiritually mature enough to be a good leader.

Today's woman carries too much responsibility on her shoulders as she struggles to play both roles in the home. This is not only wrong; it has also caused our men to weaken spiritually and grow dependent on their wives, rather than becoming the strong men of faith they are called to be.

Our sons grow up confused about their role as a man and lose respect for their fathers. The result is this: The father, feeling failure, grows paralyzed and then either emotionally or physically abandons his family, leaving them without a leader or protector. The wife, overwhelmed by all the responsibility she has to carry, takes up the role of spiritual leadership. It is neither God's intention nor His perfect plan for marriage.

We can teach our sons what it takes to become a godly leader in their homes by teaching them the husband and wife roles according to God's design. Our Lord set a perfect example of godly leadership for our men to follow. He served us, He sacrificed his own desires for us, He loved us unconditionally, He taught us how to live, He came to our rescue, He lived out His faith in front of us, and He gave up His life for us. He also commands our husbands in Ephesians 5:25 that they must do the same for their wives: "Husbands, love your wives, just as Christ loved the church and gave himself up for her" (NIV).

What woman would not want to submit to and be led by a man who takes care of her by…

- ❧ providing for her?
- ❧ serving her?
- ❧ protecting her and her children?
- ❧ leading her by example, not force?
- ❧ loving her as Christ loved the church?

Any man who has learned to lead by love and a godly example, sacrificing his own wants and desires for the well-being and protection of his family, deserves to be followed and is a rare treasure in today's society.

The truth is, women desire for their husbands to be the captain of the ship, the protector when life's storms hit. No woman really wants to lead a man. Those who do lead end up losing respect for their husbands. Those marriages usually fail because the husband loses sight of his God-appointed position and his wife, overwhelmed by responsibility, resents him for not taking care of her heart. The only way we are going to teach our sons the art of godly leadership is to stop pretending this is okay—because it is not!

We can prepare our sons to assume their God-appointed position in their own homes someday by clearing up the confusion and teaching our sons the correct male/female roles in a home, as established from the beginning by God Himself.

## Life Happens

There is nothing worse than not knowing where you are going and killing yourself to get there.

*There is nothing worse than not knowing where you are going and killing yourself to get there.*

I grew up with a dad who was always in a hurry. He led his family in fast-forward. He always had places to go, people to see, and a schedule to keep. Dad used to tell me, "Sheri, I'm fighting time. Let's go now, or I am going to bust a gut!"

One particular memory stands out above the rest. Dad was driving me to school on his way to a business meeting when all of a sudden I started my period. My dad, freaked out that he now had to stop at the store and fearing he would miss his appointment, careened across five lanes on the freeway like a maniac on wheels. He raced into the store, pushing the wrong way through the automatic swinging door, then grabbed the manager and demanded that he lead him to the feminine products aisle.

As he approached the checkout counter, in line before him stood a sweet little old lady with what seemed like five hundred coupons to redeem. She was nearing her last few coupons when my high-speed father had had enough: He grabbed the coupons from the cashier and ripped them into tiny pieces, then threw down a hundred-dollar bill, screaming, "Get out of my way, lady, I am fighting time!"

I was totally embarrassed (but secretly relieved that at least the poor lady received free groceries in exchange for her humiliation).

The point is that my father's fast-forward living trained me to eat fast, talk fast, and pack my schedule to capacity with little room for bathroom breaks or even sleep.

Some days my husband Steve will come home and say, "What did you do today?"

"I was so busy!" I'll reply exhaustedly.

"Well, what did you do?" he'll ask.

"I have no idea. But I was busy doing it!"

Steve, on the other hand, actually *chews* his food before swallowing it. He knows how to sit and talk at the same time. He takes the time to think and pray before he makes a decision. Needless to say, when we first married I was completely unequipped to follow his slower pace. I simply did not know that life had any pace other than full speed!

Since Steve did not move at the pace I was used to, I thought he could not lead me. So what did I do? I took control of the wheel…and drove us both crazy. After seven years of rushing him through life and seven years of him trying to please his fast-forward bride, I crashed and burned by passing out while speaking before a group of ladies. I was diagnosed with Epstein-Barr, a virus that breaks down your immune system and is usually brought on by stress and a lack of rest. I was stuck in bed for over six weeks; I guess God had to throw me into park to get my attention.

Due to my sickness, my wonderful husband finally got the chance to assume his rightful position as the leader of our marriage and home. Today I understand that my husband is wise for not rushing into everything, and that he is very capable of leading if I will just get out of his way and give him a chance. I also learned the hard way that if the devil can't make us bad, his next trick is to make us busy.

 *If the devil can't make us bad, his next trick is to make us busy.*

## A Mother's Influence

We should not be training our sons to depend solely on us. Instead, while they are at home we should be teaching them to become loving leaders.

As mothers, we tend to do everything for our sons because we love them and believe it is our maternal right. But if you are not careful, your son will look for a mother figure in a wife rather than a woman he can lead. Everyone knows a mama's boy does not make a good husband. It is important to be close to your son, but it is just as important to let him learn to do things for the family.

> *If you are not careful, your son will look for a mother figure in a wife rather than a woman he can lead.*

## A Mother in Action

### Ages 3–8

Start teaching your son now to serve and lead his family. I know it is tempting to do everything for him, but the first five years can set up bad habits for life. At this age, his mind is like a sponge. Your words and example are your most powerful tools. A boy needs to see himself as a leader in order to become one.

1. **Have him pray.** Encourage him to pray for the meal at dinnertime, for safety before a trip, or that God would send him a divine appointment.
2. **Read to him.** Teach him about leaders in the Bible like Moses, who sacrificed his own comfort to rescue a nation, or Noah, who followed God's call and saved his family from the flood. After you read the Bible story, engage him in discussion about what made the Bible hero a good leader.
3. **Affirm him now.** While he is young, tell him often what a great leader he will be in his home if he takes care of his family.
4. **Talk about soldiers.** Boys generally take great interest in soldiers. Talk about how a soldier's responsibility is like a husband's role in the home: to guide, to keep them safe, and to serve their country the way fathers are to serve their families.
5. **Define your role in his life.** Teach him that God's desire is for him to become a great husband and father someday, and that it is your privilege and honor to teach him what that means.

*Ages 9–13*

This is a great time to put some leadership responsibilities in place. Continue the above and add the following:

1. **Let him pray for you.** Nothing will grow a boy into a spiritual leader more than becoming a prayer warrior for his family. Teach him to cover his mom in prayer; he will someday cover his wife in the same way.

2. **Have him read the Word to you.** Reading the Word to him is important, but it will become even more real if you have *him* read it to *you.* Set a time at night or in the morning—whatever best fits your schedule.

3. **Let him help with the grocery planning.** Talk to him about how much you budget for groceries every month; then have him help you draw up your grocery list, prioritizing by nutrition and balancing that against what you can afford.

4. **Let him serve you.** Teach him that leaders serve their families by asking him to help around the house or cook dinner occasionally.

5. **Let him sacrifice for his family.** How many men today put their family at the bottom of their list of priorities without realizing it? Have your son give up something he wants to do once in a while just to help his family. Teach him now that a real man puts his family's comfort and well-being before his own.

1. **Celebrate his "coming of age."** Make a big deal out of his fourteenth birthday! In Jewish tradition, families have a bar mitzvah when the sons enter their teens; this age symbolizes entry into manhood. Tell him that he is becoming a man, and you want to give him some grown-up responsibilities and privileges.

2. **Let him participate in working out family issues.** Ask for his ideas and input regarding better ways to run the family. This does not mean relinquishing your role as a parent; rather, you are encouraging him to start thinking like a man.

3. **Let him teach the Word.** Have him prepare a devotion to teach the family once a week at the dinner table or before bedtime.

4. **Let him write the checks.** Once a week, have him sit with you and pay the bills. In this way he will learn about the financial responsibilities involved in running a household.

5. **Let him be a hero.** When he comes to your rescue in some practical way—changing a flat tire, for instance, or fixing something around the house that is broken—be sure to praise the results and reward his efforts.

6. **Help him tune in to you.** Teach him to ask you daily, "How can I help you, Mom?" before he leaves to hang

out with his friends. This trains him to be tuned in to his wife's needs someday, which will greatly impact his marriage.

## The Big Picture

The man *(the husband)* is designed to be the captain of his family's ship, and the wife *(the God-appointed helpmate)* is meant to be the radar. Many times the wife can see trouble ahead before the man, because she is more tuned in to matters of the heart. However, it is the husband's God-given responsibility to guide his family through troubled waters.

A smart man will listen to his wife's warnings, and a smart woman will give her husband time to turn the ship around. While she waits, she prays him through the storm and asks God to grant her leader wisdom as he looks for a way to get his family safely back to shore.

> *Even the Son of Man did not come to be served.*
> *Instead, he came to serve others.*
> *He came to give his life as the price for*
> *setting many people free.*
>
> MARK 10:45, NIRV

*A Mother's Prayer*

❧

*Dear God,*
*Give my son the desire to become*
*a godly leader. Grant me divine wisdom*
*in raising him to lead a family someday.*
*Please help me remember that I am*
*raising someone else's husband.*
*I pray for his wife, wherever she is,*
*that she will be his perfect helpmate*
*and will desire to let him lead her.*
*In Your name I pray, amen.*

# chapter twelve

# Teach Him to Be Accountable

*If one falls down, his friend can help him up.*
*But pity the man who falls and has*
*no one to help him up!*

Ecclesiastes 4:10, NIV

Every day we hear about great men who sacrificed their families, their witness, their character, and everything they worked to achieve for a few fleeting moments' pleasure.

As we see in the Bible, even King David—who had enough strength to walk out onto a battlefield without any armor and kill a giant—was not strong enough to resist the temptation of another man's wife. David was called "a man after God's own heart," but even he was tripped up by temptation and fell into the dreaded pit of adultery.

We would be fools to teach our sons that this could never

happen to them. Yes, our boys are called to lead and become mighty warriors in the land; however, they cannot do it alone.

When it comes to weakness for women, men are no different today than back in the Bible days. Look at the utter devastation of so many American families because men did not surround themselves with fellow warriors who were committed to protecting one another's purity. Too many men think they can go it alone.

Often, the more a man loves God, the more he distances himself from accountability. He may as well paint a big red target on his chest. Claims like "That could never happen to me" or "I am stronger than that" are usually the last boastful words uttered before the enemy sets his sights and pulls the trigger.

## Life Happens

John and Marie fell deeply in love in college. Both had big dreams about furthering God's kingdom, and they were excited to do it together.

Over the years God blessed them with all they had ever imagined: a thriving church, two beautiful children, a happy marriage, and an effective ministry. They were one of the most respected couples in the community. It was evident that they loved God with all their hearts.

One day John was busy at work in his church office when a young lady burst through the doors, crying hysterically. Struggling to catch her breath, she told John about her desperate attempts to escape from her abusive husband. The police had done nothing to help in the past, and she was sure he would kill her if he found her. John quickly called Marie to take the young lady to a safe place. That afternoon Marie helped this desperate, broken young woman gather her kids and some clothes. Marie then brought them to the safety of her and John's home.

Over the next few days, several of John's trusted staff offered to step in and help. But John felt that the young lady needed more than protection; she needed the Lord, and he and Marie were the people to lead her to Him. Sure enough, in a matter of days, Marie and John's love for this young woman led her to become a Christian.

After spending a few weeks in their home, she was like a new person—both hungry for God and at peace. John and Marie were delighted to have made such an impact on this young woman and her kids.

During the weeks this woman and her children stayed in John and Marie's home, the church leaders approached John several times about having the woman move out and stay with another single mom. His response was, "Marie is really helping her. I can't ask her to leave now; she may fall away from the Lord."

Somewhere along the line, while John was trying to minister to and protect this woman from harm, he forgot to protect himself and his own family. His good intentions, minus the necessary accountability, left him wide open and unguarded.

One fateful night temptation took its toll. John was home alone with the woman while Marie attended a Bible study. Marie walked into her home to find John and the young woman in bed together.

One strong man of faith left himself wide open for one moment of weakness, and it wiped out his whole world. All he had lived for and loved was destroyed in a matter of weeks, due to an unprotected marriage and not listening to the warning of appointed leaders in the church.

*One strong man of faith left himself wide open for one moment of weakness, and it wiped out his whole world.*

Unable to handle the guilt of what he had done, John left his family and his church and married the young woman. Two years into his new marriage, however, he was diagnosed with acute leukemia and given only ten weeks to live. Sadly, his new young wife decided she did not want to take care of a sick old man; she emptied his bank account and left him alone—with no family, no children, no loving church body, and nothing to show for his years of hard work and dedication to ministry.

And yet as tragic as this story is, the ending is redeeming. You see, Marie did something extraordinary for her ex-husband. She decided that John's last days on earth should be free of guilt and shame, and she went to him—not gloating with condemnation, but offering him love and mercy. She took care of him, never leaving his bedside, until he drew his last breath. Marie gave John an amazing final gift: forgiveness.

How differently John's legacy could have played out if he had listened to the wisdom of his elders (his accountability). If only he had recognized that he was not strong enough to stay home alone with a young, vulnerable woman—no matter what the circumstances.

I can't help but wonder… If John's mother could have foreseen his future, would she have warned him that he would end up on the enemy's hit list unless he surrounded himself with strong, mighty men to hold him accountable?

## A Mother's Influence

Accountability is the key to locking in the blessed life God desires for our sons. What a tragedy it would be if we dedicated our lives to preparing them to love their wives and lead their families, yet forgot to teach them accountability!

We are setting our boys up for failure if we let them think they are not susceptible to temptation. They must be taught at a young age that they cannot do life alone. The Bible says temptation will come—that even Jesus was tempted. King

David sinned with Bathsheba because he was alone, unaccountable, and not where he was supposed to be.

Accountability and humility go hand in hand. Proverbs warns us that pride comes before a fall, and Ecclesiastes 4:12 says one man can be overpowered, two can defend themselves, but a strand of three is not easily broken. As mothers, we need to point our sons toward the kinds of friends who will help them stay strong in their walk with God.

But it doesn't end there. We also need to teach them how to recognize which friends are good accountability partners and which are not. When they are grown, they'll be selecting their own friends. If they have learned to pray for and seek out fellow warriors in the fight, accountability will become a shield of protection for them and their families.

## A Mother in Action

*Ages 3–8*
It is never too early to start forming good habits with your son, especially when it comes to accountability. Obviously, your son will not struggle with sexual temptation at this age. But boys think they can do things alone—they like the thrill of not depending on anyone or anything.

Encouraging your son's independence ("I can do it all by myself") and self-discipline ("I only need one piece of candy") is great for developing strong leaders. However, your little warrior needs to recognize that there are battles he

Preparing Him for the Other Woman

should not go into alone, and that it's important he have friends to encourage and hold him accountable.

1. **Be selective about the friends you allow him to play with.** Remember, we become like those we surround ourselves with. If there is a task to do, encourage them to help each other.
2. **Take advantage of teachable moments.** When he disobeys you, or if he hurts himself or someone else, talk about the consequences of disobedience.
3. **Talk with him about how we all fall down if we do not have someone to help us.** Talk about the dangers of not doing things God's way, and openly discuss the difference between adventure and unsafe risks that could hurt him.
4. **Teach him to repent.** When he is in the wrong, emphasize the importance of repentance. Turn to God quickly, and then pray with your son for the strength to walk away from temptation and for friends to help him stay strong in his faith.

### Ages 9–13
Continue all the above on accountability and add the following:

1. **Keep a close watch on your son.** Too many moms grow lenient at this age and do not keep a close eye on their boys. They are not streetwise, and the friends they keep

during this age can make or break how successfully they begin their teen years. So keep an eye on how your son is affected by his peers.

2. **Set boundaries.** Part of the key to accountability is to teach him to set boundaries for himself. Since he is still too young to discern what he can and cannot handle all the time, for now you will have to continue doing that for him. Write out the boundaries you and your son discuss so he can review them occasionally.

3. **Ask questions.** Make him accountable for his plans before he goes somewhere. Ask questions like who will be there and how long he will be gone, and set a time for him to check in. This will help him remain accountable for his actions.

4. **Meet the parents.** Do not let your son wander into the enemy's trap. Meet the parents of his friends and check out the homes of the places your son hangs out. Too many parents have no idea what kind of homes their boys are walking into.

5. **Pray with him.** Before he walks out your door, pray for God to keep him strong. Talk to him when you see a situation that could hurt him or his witness. This will help give him spiritual insight on his choices.

6. **Do not make excuses for him.** Part of accountability is helping him learn to take responsibility for his actions. Excuses will not help him in any way grow into a man of God.

7. **Let him know you trust him.** If you tell him that you trust him, he will be more motivated to be trustworthy. Use affirming words to bolster him—this is an effective tool for growing him into a man of character.

### Ages 14–19
Continue all the above and add the following:

1. **Invite his friends into your home.** Have his friends over at your home often so you can connect and observe who is influencing him. Open your home for a small group from his youth group or for weekly movie and game nights. Come up with some fun themes like "breakfast for dinner" or pizza night.
2. **Connect before he leaves.** Your connection to your son is a major key to his accountability. Don't let him walk out the door without looking you in the eye and letting him know that you are praying for him. Although it is important for him to share his plans (where he is going and who he'll be with), let him know that you trust him to make the right decisions.

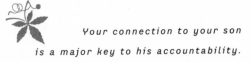

*Your connection to your son is a major key to his accountability.*

3. **Help him stand in the gap.** When he tells you one of his friends is struggling with drinking or a relationship with a girl, encourage him to go talk to his friend before he or she falls. Placing him in a position of leadership with his friends adds to his own accountability.

4. **Inspire him to dream.** Talk to him about his goals and dreams. Remind him that God has a vision for his life; this will place a desire in his heart to succeed. Many of the men who fall do so because they lose sight of their original dreams and goals.

5. **Put a godly fear in him.** Jesus used a lot of parables to help His followers grasp the concept of godliness. Share with your son real-life scenarios that remind him to be on his guard. Remind him that we're all only one choice away from life-changing consequences.

6. **Talk about his future bride.** Remind him that if he remains pure now, he is training himself to remain faithful in his marriage. And he will be blessed on his honeymoon by giving himself only to his wife.

7. **Finish strong.** If your son is ever tempted to fall, it will be in his teen years. So stay alert and prayed up, because you are his accountability now.

## The Big Picture

We have all seen the devastating effects of infidelity and the broken life of a godly man who has fallen into the enemy's trap. How many marriages would still be standing if some-one were there to stop the fall? If men would humble themselves enough to say, *I need someone to stop me from destroying all I love for a moment's pleasure?*

> *How many marriages would still be standing if someone were there to stop the fall?*

We can do our part to rebuild the foundation of America's family by training our sons to be accountable to others. We can prepare them for the battles of the mind and the temptation of the flesh by giving them the spiritual weapons to win the war against infidelity and fatherless families.

Pray that your son will remain faithful to love his future wife, fulfill his God-given call, and complete the work he was destined to do on earth.

> *If you think you are standing strong, be careful, for you, too, may fall into the same sin.*
>
> 1 CORINTHIANS 10:12, NLT

## A Mother's Prayer

Dear God,

Help my son walk in humility
with a godly fear.
Give him friends and accountability
partners who will keep him from
falling into the enemy's trap.
Grant me wisdom to raise him up
to be a mighty warrior for Your kingdom.
And give him ears to hear and eyes to
see the warning signs before it is too late.
In Your name I pray, amen.

# chapter thirteen

# Teach Him to Find a Good Wife

*A worthy wife is her husband's joy and crown; a shameful wife saps his strength.*

PROVERBS 12:4, NLT

$\mathcal{C}$an you imagine spending years preparing your beloved boy to become a godly husband, only to see him end up marrying the wrong woman because he was never taught how to look for a good wife?

Before I began writing this chapter, I went deep into the Word to glean as much wisdom as possible from the Creator of marriage, God the Father. What I discovered revealed some major shifts between marriage as it was originally created and what it has become. One of the greatest differences I saw was that in the beginning God used parents to help find good wives for their sons.

Marriage has suffered much because our society has forgotten that it was God's idea, not man's. That it is a lifelong covenant, not a mere convenience. That it is a supernatural union, not a superficial partnership. It is between a man and a woman, both created uniquely to be equal, yet vastly different in the roles of husband and wife.

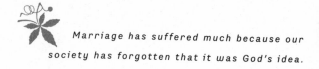

*Marriage has suffered much because our society has forgotten that it was God's idea.*

This is not an area of your son's life that you should let him learn the hard way. Aside from his decision to follow God, the most important choice your prince will make is which young lady will take that long walk down the aisle and join him at the wedding altar. Who will his princess be?

## Life Happens

I have always been in love with the idea of love. Like most women, I spent much of my single life dreaming about the day I would finally meet my prince. I imagined countless scenarios of the proposal—how I would feel, and what he would do to woo me.

As a result, my first engagement was tender and roman-

Preparing Him for the Other Woman

tic and wonderful. So was my second. And my third!

Even more memorable was the fact they all sort of...overlapped.

Now, before you judge me too harshly, hear my story. When I was in my twenties, I produced modeling and talent shows in different cities throughout the U.S. I was on the road for weeks at a time and had the chance to meet many different types of men. (I have to admit, I truly enjoyed dating men while they were still in "marketing" mode—they were always on their best behavior!)

Well, after two years of cross-country dating, I narrowed my search to three very special young bachelors in three different cities. Each would have made a good choice for a husband. First there was Michael, the model from Phoenix—a fun, sweet, romantic college boy. Then there was David, a chiropractor from San Diego—stable, successful, able to provide comfortably (and hey, free neck adjustments for life!). Finally, there was Kyman, a carpenter from San Jose—a handsome, quiet, polite guy who always treated me like a princess.

My fiancé fiasco all began one Wednesday evening while I was with Michael at his church in Arizona. As the service came to an end, he promptly stood to his feet and proclaimed to the entire congregation that he had met the woman he was going to marry. Right then and there he got down on one knee, ring in hand, and proposed.

Now, how was I supposed to say no to that? Besides, we were in a church! *It must be a God thing,* I thought.

A few weeks later, I was in San Diego trying to break the news to Bachelor #2, David the chiropractor. My plan to drop the bomb over dinner was not going well, however. I kept trying to work the subject of my engagement into the conversation, but David wasn't making it easy for me.

As I sat there, doubts about Michael began floating through my mind. After all, I really did want a mature and stable man. Michael was a model/student/dreamer. Sure, he was cute and fun and romantic, but the security David offered was also important to me. Oh, if only David could take a few tips from Michael! It was a tough call.

That night, however, I saw a new side to David—he was charming, laughing, completely at ease. We were having so much fun!

*What does this mean? Is David the one?* I wondered.

No sooner had that thought gone through my mind when, sure enough, David reached into his pocket and pulled out an engagement ring. "I love you, Sheri Rose, and I want to marry you," he said. Choking back tears, he continued, "I've never said these words to anyone before in my life. I waited to say them until I met the woman I knew I would spend my life with."

I melted into the moment, basking in his sincerity and this romantic side to him that had never before surfaced.

Then a light went on in my head. *God must be rescuing me from marrying Michael!* I thought. *What else could this possibly mean?*

"Yes, David!" I blurted. "I will marry you!"

Okay, I did leave out the tiny detail that I was, in fact, already engaged. But surely God would work *that* out.

Over the next few days I screened countless calls from Michael and David on my answering machine. I had no strength to pick up the phone. I just stood there paralyzed, clutching two engagement rings in my sweaty palms.

I decided that I needed to get away from the stress and figure out what I was supposed to do. So I hopped on a plane to San Jose to visit Kyman the carpenter. Now, an interesting piece of background about our relationship is that Kyman's grandparents were the missionaries who led me to the Lord. Their marriage was so beautiful that it drew me like a magnet to the kingdom of God. I always felt safe and cared for when I was with them, and their grandson Kyman had the same calming effect on my crazy world. I loved that he never put any pressure on me, and I fit into his family so well. There wasn't much "electricity" in our relationship, but at this point in my life I just needed peace—not passion.

While I was in San Jose, Kyman and I relaxed at the beach, worked out together, and went out to dinner like the best of friends. It was all so relaxed and stress-free; I never wanted our time together to end. But the weekend came to a screeching halt while Kyman was driving me to the airport to return home. With uncharacteristic boldness, he said, "Would you ever consider marrying me, Sheri Rose?"

Now, keep in mind that I was already in shock. That's the

*only* way to explain why saying yes to the third man in three weeks made any sense to me!

What was I thinking? I did not need another fiancé. What I needed was to be locked up until I could make a choice. During my flight home, as I clutched two engagement rings and with a third promised, I broke down and cried out to God for help.

When I stepped off that plane, I knew what I had to do. Mustering all my strength and sanity, I called each man and told him that I needed some time to think things over. (Did I ever!)

I decided to throw myself into my work and go produce another event in San Francisco with my best friend, Joyce. For the next few weeks I worked twelve-hour days, studiously avoiding the phone calls pouring in from my three suitors.

Meanwhile, Michael, being the aggressive, adventurous type, decided to hop on a plane and come surprise me on the final night of the show I was producing. If you think that idea might have culminated in one very awkward scenario, you'd be right. Now try multiplying it by three! That's right, David and Kyman also had the bright idea to come and surprise me on that fateful night.

There I was, backstage with 120 performers, waiting for the curtain to go up. Joyce peeked through the curtain to survey the packed audience. Suddenly her face turned white. "You'll have to get down on your knees for this one," she whispered frantically. "Maybe even try fasting."

"What are you talking about?" I asked anxiously, know-

Preparing Him for the Other Woman

ing the curtain was going up in less than a minute.

She practically jerked my arm off as she led me to the small slit in the curtain at center stage. "See any familiar faces out there?" she asked.

I shook my head.

"How about front row, right there in the center?"

As the house lights started to dim, I focused on the three seats front and center. *No way,* I thought. *I must be hallucinating.*

Sure enough, there they were sitting side by side in the front row: Michael, David, and Kyman—my three fiancés, strangers to one another, lined up like birds on a fence.

Nothing in my life could have prepared me for having the three men I had promised to marry show up unannounced at the same time in the same place.

No sooner had my jaw dropped than the curtain came up. There I was—nowhere to run, nowhere to hide. The mess I had made had caught up with me at last. My hands began to shake, and the skin on my neck glowed red hot. Sweat began slipping down my back, soaking my gown like a workout T-shirt. My lips quivered, and I could barely pronounce the names of the contestants and their sponsors.

I stood there on the stage like a deer in the headlights. Each of my men proudly smiled at me, oblivious of the other two. All I could wonder was how in the world I would ever explain this one. *Maybe God will spare me the embarrassment and strike me dead right now!* I thought.

As the end of the show drew near, I nearly began hyper-ventilating backstage. Joyce handed me a paper bag to breathe into. My heart was pounding out of control, and my whole chest was so tight it hurt. When I went onstage at the close of the show, I noticed Michael turn to the other two and point at me. I couldn't hear his words, but he was obviously telling them, "That's the girl I'm going to marry."

In a split second, all three of their smiles disappeared. What replaced them were expressions of astonishment, betrayal, confusion, and anger. I realized the show was over—in more ways than one. God finally had my attention.

Through that fiasco I learned the hard way that choosing a mate is not a game to play, but a life to share. Love is about finding someone who draws you closer to God, not someone who takes the place of God.

Those three good men each became wiser for the decision to leave me!

## A Mother's Influence

Talk often to your son about the kind of woman who would be best for him. Seek the Lord together in prayer, emphasizing that a marriage needs to have God as the key ingredient.

Whether you are married or a single mom, try to treat men with honor and respect before your son. Remember, the way you treat your son and the way you treat men in front of him will have a big impact on the kind of woman he looks for. He will grow up to become a better leader if he knows that being a godly husband to a supportive, loving wife is one of the highest callings he will have in life.

## A Mother in Action

*Ages: Toddler to Teen*

The time is now. While your son is still young and under your influence, you can instill wisdom in him when it comes to finding a good wife. Whenever you read a book together, watch a movie, or encounter a real-life situation, point out to him women who are examples of both good and bad wives.

1.  **Pray for your son's wife with him.** By praying for her in front of him and talking to him about the qualities to look for in a godly wife, you are cementing a prosperous future for your son. Remind him that choosing a wife is the most important decision he will ever make, and encourage him to pray for his wife now. He may not be able now to grasp the idea of being a husband, but you are planting seeds that will grow later in his life.

    Remember, he is at an age when he trusts you about everything. You can have an amazing impact on your son and his future bride if you commit her to the Lord.

*Encourage him to pray for his wife now.*

2. **Have him journal.** When he is eighteen or nineteen, buy him a journal for his future wife. Write a simple prayer in the journal before you give it to him, then encourage him to begin writing prayers and letters to his bride. This will teach him about expressing love through words. It will also get him in the habit of thinking about his future wife, since writing out one's thoughts makes them more real. You may even want to ask him if you could write a letter to your future daughter-in-law in the journal.

3. **Stay tuned in to your son.** If you remain keyed in to his thoughts and emotions, he will in turn remain open to your input. He needs to see the benefits of a woman who truly loves him and God. Believe me, your son is making many mental notes that will prove helpful to him when he begins looking for a wife.

4. **Take note of your son's growing attraction to girls.** When he starts noticing girls, encourage him to start thinking about the kind of woman he wants to marry. Talk about the qualities and temperaments of the different types of girls he likes and dislikes. Ask questions like, "What kind of mother do you think she will be?" "What is her family like?" "How is her relationship with God?" "Does she inspire you to be a better person when you're with her?" These questions will really help your son focus on the big picture.

# The Big Picture

I've seen too many of my dear friends run into the arms of the wrong person out of rebellion to either God or their parents. Tragically, many of them have paid a huge price for their poor choice, and so did their children.

God's plan is for marriage to be a covenant between two people who are "equally yoked." That means following the same path and serving the same master. Just take a close look at the failed marriages around you. How many of those marriages began with partners who held different values and different faiths, despite warnings from friends and families?

You can help your son desire more than a pretty face or a strong personality to conquer. Marriage is challenging enough with the right person, but it can become like a life-long prison sentence with the wrong person. Do not let your guard down when it comes to protecting your son from becoming unequally yoked. Use your God-given influence to help him choose a good wife so he can have the good life and walk in favor with God, as promised in Proverbs 18:22.

> *Live happily with the woman you love through all the meaningless days of life that God has given you in this world. The wife God gives you is your reward for all your earthly toil.*
>
> ECCLESIASTES 9:9, NLT

## A Mother's Prayer

~

Dear God,
I pray for my son's wife, wherever she is.
I ask You to protect my boy from making
the wrong choice when it is time for him
to choose a wife. Give him Your wisdom,
and open his eyes to Your perfect will
for him and his partner for life.
Protect him from pursuing a counterfeit.
Lead him to long for You first, so that he
will be available when You bring him a
woman who loves You with all her heart
and who completes him as a man.
In Your name I pray, amen.

# chapter fourteen

# Prepare Yourself for
# the Other Woman

*I* recently wrote a book entitled *My Prince Will Come: Preparing for the Lord's Return.* I love dreaming about Jesus' return and what heaven will be like. My heart's desire is to be totally prepared for that great day.

While I am still on earth, however, I'm not sure anything will really prepare me for the day another woman joins my son at the altar—officially replacing me as the woman in his life. I'm pretty sure I'll be shedding tears of both joy and sadness, considering the endless hours and countless prayers I've invested in my boy and his bride-to-be. What an honor it will be to finally meet the girl I have been praying for since the day my son was born!

I think that letting go of our little boys—watching them become men, placing them into the arms of the other woman—is the most difficult part about being a mother. My eyes well up as I both dread and dream about the day Jake chooses a wife.

Perhaps you, like me, experience a wide array of emotions as we ask ourselves the following questions:

- "How will I feel when I am no longer the only woman in my son's life?"
- "How will I fit into his life once he is married?"
- "What will my daughter-in-law be like?"
- "Will she love Jake as much as I do?"
- "Will she appreciate all the time, training, and effort I put into preparing him to be her husband?"

And the more important questions to ask ourselves:

- "What kind of mother-in-law will I be?"
- "What can I do to prepare my heart to love and accept her?"

There seem to be a lot of unknowns in exchange for years of praying and preparing our sons for that moment. However, as difficult as it will be to release my son to the world, I still take comfort in knowing the One who holds his future and mine. I know I can trust Him with my beloved boy's life, and I know I was chosen to be Jake's mother for the purpose of preparing him to love a wife and lead a family.

Although I do not know what Jake will walk through in this life, I do know my God is faithful—that He never breaks His promises to His children. Knowing these things gives me the ability to enjoy my new role in my son's life as his friend, his counselor, and—someday—as mother to my new daughter-in-law.

## Life Happens

After my escapade with the three "wise men" (they were wise for leaving me!), I decided to wait on God to reveal my future husband. I chose instead to devote myself to my real Prince, the Lover of my soul, Jesus.

One year later, God brought me His choice of a husband in a supernatural way.

Steve was different from any man I had ever dated. He had never even had a girlfriend before, and was not a Casanova kind of guy who knew all the right words and moves to "get the girl." The truth is, I felt *closer* to God when I was with Steve.

There were no fireworks at first, just a comfortable relationship between a man and a woman who both loved the Lord. But after three months of working, praying, and playing together, I fell in love—this time in a very different way.

However, I was unsure how Steve felt about me. Then one evening he asked me to come to his hotel room, where he was staying during the show we were producing. Now, when most guys invite a girl into a hotel room, it is for one reason. However, Steve had a different agenda than most men. He did not want to sleep with me; he wanted to marry me.

When I walked into the room, there was Christian praise music playing and a beautifully set table in the middle of the room with three candles—two of them lit. He took my hand and led me to one of the chairs, then knelt beside me, bowed his head, and prayed for God's guidance in our relationship and His blessing on our future together. He then served me my first Communion and asked me to marry him. And when he spoke the words, "Will you marry me?" I knew this time the question came straight from the Lord.

I said, "Yes!" and we kissed for the first time. He then had us light the middle candle together, signifying the joining of two into one, ignited by the very Spirit of God. There was an indescribable sense that God Himself was in the room with us, whispering, "I chose both of you. This marriage is My idea. It's My perfect plan for you."

I guess God knew that I needed divine intervention. How else could I explain my new fiancé to my friends and family? Breaking the news to Steve's family would be quite a different story. Steve's upbringing and mine were like night and day. I was raised to think that boyfriends were like underpants (you should never be caught without 'em!). And as I said, Steve had never had a girlfriend. Maybe I should underscore the word *never!* He had been on dates before, but his parents had never heard their son utter the phrase, "Mom and Dad, I'd like you to meet my girlfriend."

So how does a son break the news that he's engaged to a girl his parents have never met? Well, he decided that, rather than tell his family over the phone that he had met and proposed to a glamour girl from Southern California after knowing her for just eight weeks, it would be more fun to see their faces by surprising them at his grandparents' fiftieth wedding anniversary, to be held at his uncle's farm in North Dakota.

Having been raised by a wealthy Jewish father from Hollywood, I had a mental image of a farm: an extravagant country estate, complete with Mercedes convertible, elegant dinner parties, radiant hosts, servants, private jets, and Olympic-size swimming pools. (If you recall the popular 1980s TV show *Dallas*, you'd be on the right track.)

So with my mental image firmly lodged in my mind, I was determined to make the right impression by looking my best. You can imagine the type of attire I selected for my first meeting with my future in-laws. Let me paint you a picture: designer embroidered bright-white jumpsuit with big shoulder pads and massive amounts of rhinestones; big, dangly earrings; a gigantic, sparkly silver briefcase of a purse; tall white rhinestone-encrusted boots; huge, teased hair; and nails an inch long with even more rhinestones glued on. And if that was not enough glam, add in my false eyelashes and the maximum amount of makeup and perfume allowed by the law.

Let's just say you could smell *and* see me coming from a mile away.

When I checked in at the airport, the metal detectors went into frenzy as I attempted to get my big hair and pounds of rhinestones through the security gate. Everyone was staring at me—which I actually thought was a good thing, since my goal was to capture the attention of my future family.

I will never forget the look on Steve's face as his future bride got off the plane, covered in blinding rhinestones and with rock-hard hair.

"How do I look?" I asked. "Do you think your parents will think I am pretty enough for their son?" (Though I'm ashamed to admit it now, I'm pretty sure I batted my eyelashes at this point.)

Steve just stood there, speechless, trying to figure out a polite way to tell me we were not going to JR's estate on *Dallas*. We were going to a humble country farm in the middle of No-Man's-Land, North Dakota, and we would not be picked up by a limo but, rather, crammed in the back of his parents' truck for two hours to get there.

This was all a far cry from what I had imagined in my head, but I still wanted to make a good impression. So I ignored his gentle warning and went on my merry way to catch our next plane together.

The moment finally arrived when I would meet the man and woman who raised my husband-to-be. As I followed Steve off the plane, he had me hide behind him to make a memorable impression. I'm sure his parents were probably wondering who the wild woman was peeking out from behind their son.

Then Steve brought me forward, threw his arms around my waist, and said, "Mom, Dad, I want you to meet your future daughter-in-law!"

They were surprised, all right; in fact, their expressions were definitely worthy of a Kodak moment. In essence, I was everything that Steve and his family were not, and his family was everything I had wanted while I was growing up. We needed each other.

Today my mother-in-law tells her friends that I put color in her black-and white-world. In return, I love my mother-in-law beyond words and consider her one of my best friends. Although we were nothing alike, we completed each other. More important, we loved and served the same God. In fact, we compare ourselves to Naomi and Ruth in the Bible, because I would follow her anywhere (except Arizona in the summertime…but that's another story).

Sometimes I think I would have married Steve just to become her daughter.

## Future Mother-in-Law in Action

Years ago my husband and I were speaking at a church together. I was sharing with the congregation how I wasn't raised in a Christian home and that as a young girl I didn't have a mom who prayed for me. In the middle of my story, my husband politely interrupted me and took the microphone.

*This had better be good,* I thought.

"Sheri Rose, you're mistaken," Steve said. "You *did* have a mother who prayed for you. My mother has prayed for my wife-to-be ever since I was a little boy! Even though she didn't know who you were, she prayed for you."

That startling realization still makes me cry every time I think of it…in fact, I'm crying even now, as I write! To think that a woman I had never met approached her King in prayer with *me* in her heart and on her lips.

What an awesome privilege it is to pray for your son's future wife.

## Journal to Your Future Daughter-in-Law

Buy a pretty journal and begin to write encouraging letters and prayers to your future daughter-in-law. I can promise you that if you do this, you will begin to fall in love with her before you ever meet her. As a result, the transition will be much easier when it happens.

## Start a Hope Chest for Her

Can you imagine how she will feel if you present her with a hope chest filled with photos, the journal you have been writing in since your son was a little boy, and some special keepsakes? It is possible that you will be the only mother she ever knows who does something special like that for her.

Remember, you're raising her husband. As hard as this thought is for me, I choose to make myself think about it often. Among other benefits, it truly helps me to continue preparing my son to be a husband.

## A Mother's Prayer
## for Her Daughter-in-Law

∽

Dear God,

Prepare me to love my future

daughter-in-law.

Give me a heart that welcomes

her into our family. Help me to do my

part to prepare my son to be her husband,

and help me to release my beloved

boy to her when the time is right.

In Your name I pray, amen.

## My Closing Prayer for You

*Dear heavenly Father,*

*Give Your daughter the strength and wisdom*

*to be preparing her son for his future bride.*

*Please meet her every need and grant her the*

*secret desires of her heart. Be her provider,*

*her comfort, and her prince. May she experience*

*Your love in such a way that her life will*

*reflect that she is Your Princess,*

*a daughter of the King!*

*In Your name I pray, amen.*

Even if I never do get to meet you in person, I look forward to celebrating our work on earth with you in heaven. Until then, may our Lord bless you in every way.

Love,

Your sister princess in Christ,

Sheri Rose

# You Are God's Masterpiec

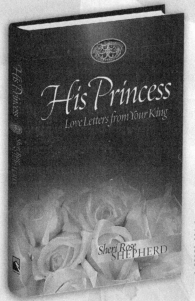

1-59052-331-8

Give yourself the gift of hearing His voice speak directly to y in these beautiful scriptural love letters from your King. Let yo soul soak in His love as each letter reminds you WHO you are WHY you are here, and HOW much you are loved.

*I have many devotional books, but very few have found their way into morning quiet-time ritual. But from the first day I began His Princess I k this was a book I wanted to read every day. Encouraging and insightfu this book reminds me how special I am to my Lord. I love this book!*
—Tricia Goyer, amazon.com revie

# The Crowning Moment

1-59052-531-0

$M$y *Prince Will Come* is the third book in the His
Princess™ series. Encouraging as it is practical, *My Prince
Will Come* equips every woman to start living today a life
of incredible freedom from the past, joy in the present,
and hope for the future.

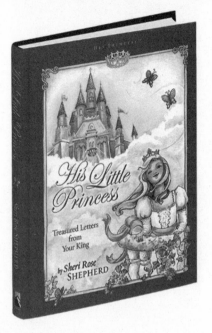